T0211937

# Trust Management in Cloud Services

Talal H. Noor • Quan Z. Sheng
Athman Bouguettaya

# Trust Management in Cloud Services

 Springer

Talal H. Noor
College of Computer Science
and Engineering
Taibah University
Yanbu
Saudi Arabia

Athman Bouguettaya
School of Computer Science
and Information Technology
RMIT University
Melbourne
Victoria
Australia

Quan Z. Sheng
School of Computer Science
The University of Adelaide
Adelaide
South Australia
Australia

ISBN 978-3-319-35934-2     ISBN 978-3-319-12250-2 (eBook)
DOI 10.1007/978-3-319-12250-2

Springer Cham Heidelberg New York Dordrecht London
© Springer International Publishing Switzerland 2014
Softcover reprint of the hardcover 1st edition 2014

Printed on acid-free paper

Springer is part of Springer Science+Business Media (www.springer.com)

*To my parents, Hashim and Amal my wife,*
*Nouran my daughter, Jood my son,*
*Abdulrahman my brothers, Hussam and Raed*
*my sisters, Wejdan and Razan.*

Talal H. Noor

*To my parents Shuilian and Jianwu, my*
*brothers Guanzheng and Xinzheng, my wife*
*Yaping and my daughters Fiona and Phoebe.*

Quan Z. Sheng

*To my wife, Malika and lovely sons, Zakaria,*
*Ayoub, and Mohamed-Islam.*

Athman Bouguettaya

# Foreword

The rapidly growing Internet-based services such as blogging, social networking, and knowledge search have substantially changed the way that users deploy, interact, communicate, and access computing resources. Cloud computing is a relatively new computing paradigm which is critical for large scale service delivery. With cloud computing, users enjoy the option to deploy their services over a network of large resource pool with practically no capital investment and modest operating cost. Cloud services promise a number of benefits such as reduced expenses and support simplicity in providing flexible and on-demand infrastructures, platforms and software as services for users.

Despite a considerable amount of benefits provided by cloud computing, the highly dynamic, distributed, and non-transparent nature of cloud services raises a number of challenges, which need to be fully addressed before promised benefits of cloud computing can be realized. Trust is widely regarded as a critical component to the success of Internet-based services. Trust is often assumed to be an implicit property that exists in the background rather than being an explicit property, which is well-defined and quantifiable. While managing trust is challenging in existing computing systems, it is much more complicated in cloud environment due to the nature of cloud services.

There is a variety of books on the market that cover interesting issues related to cloud computing. However, none but this book provides a comprehensive overview of trust management of services in cloud environments. This book is the first to provide a holistic view of the issues related to the trust management for service interactions in cloud environments. The book also covers in details fundamental technical details concerning credibility-based trust management of cloud services. Furthermore, the book reports key findings from first-hand experience in analyzing a large number of real-world cloud services. The extensive references included in this book will also help the interested readers find out more information on the discussed topics.

This book is an invaluable, topical, and timely source of knowledge in the general field of cloud computing which is suitable to a wide audience that includes advanced undergraduate students, postgraduate students, researchers, and practitioners working at the intersection of Trust, Services, and Clouds. It is a key reference for anyone interested in theory, practice and application of trust in cloud computing.

Purdue University                                                          Elisa Bertino
West Lafayette, IN, USA
August 2014

# Preface

Cloud computing is gaining a considerable momentum as a new computing paradigm for providing flexible and on-demand infrastructures, platforms and software as services. The trust management of services issues attracted many researchers in the past years. However, in cloud computing, with the highly dynamic, distributed and non-transparent nature of cloud services, this research area has gained a considerable significance. Robust trust management approaches will be essential in establishing trust between cloud service consumers and providers and will significantly contribute to the adoption and growth of cloud computing.

In this book, we present a novel approach for credibility-based trust management and automatic discovery of cloud services in distributed and highly dynamic environments. We first propose a *Zero-Knowledge Credibility Proof Protocol* to prove the credibility of consumers' feedback without breaching consumers' privacy. We then propose an adaptive and robust *Credibility Model* for assessing the consumers' credibility in giving feedback to cloud services. To measure how experienced a consumer would be, we use the concepts of *Consumer Capability* and *Majority Consensus*. We further introduce the concepts of *Feedback Density* and *Occasional Feedback Collusion* to detect strategic and occasional behaviors of collusion attacks. To detect Sybil attacks, we introduce the concepts of *Multi-Identity Recognition* and *Occasional Sybil Attacks*. To adjust trust results for cloud services that have been affected by malicious behaviors, we introduce the concept of *Change Rate of Trust*. We then propose a scalable *Availability Model* to manage the availability of the decentralized implementation of the trust management service. To share the workload between the trust management service nodes, we use the concept of *load balancing* thereby always maintaining a desired availability level. We introduce the concept of *operational power* to determine the optimal number of nodes and exploit particle filtering to precisely predict the availability of each node and determine the optimal number of replicas for each node.

The techniques presented in this book are implemented in *Cloud Armor*, a prototype that provides a set of functionalities to deliver Trust as a Service (TaaS). Finally, we conduct an exhaustive series of experimental and performance studies of the proposed techniques using a collection of real-world trust feedbacks on cloud services. We particularly develop a Cloud Service Crawler Engine for cloud services collection. The collected datasets include meta-data of nearly 6000 real-world cloud services (1.06 GB). The experimental results shows that our system (i) is able to effectively distinguish between feedbacks from experienced and amateur consumers; (ii) is more adaptive and robust in trust calculations by effectively detecting collusion and Sybil attacks without breaching consumers' privacy no matter attacks occur in a strategic or occasional behavior; (iii) is more scalable and maintains a desired availability level in highly dynamic environments and (iv) provides an efficient support for identifying, collecting, validating, categorizing and recommending cloud services based on trust.

Talal H. Noor
Quan Z. Sheng
Athman Bouguettaya

# Acknowledgements

I owe a huge debt of gratitude to my mother, my father, my wife, my daughter, my son, my brothers and my sisters who made all of this possible, for their endless love, support and patience. They have been always there for me whenever I needed them.

Talal H. Noor

I would like to sincerely thank my mum for her love.

Quan Z. Sheng

I would like thank my family for their love and understanding during my work on this book

Athman Bouguettaya

The authors of this book would like to extend their sincere gratitude and appreciation to their collaborators for the contribution to this book, in particular, we would like to mention, Anne H.H. Ngu, Schahram Dustdar, Sherali Zeadally, Zakaria Maamar, Jian Yu, Lina Yao, Abdullah Alfazi and Jeriel Law. Thank you all!

# Contents

# List of Figures

.

# List of Tables

# Chapter 1
# Introduction

Over the past few years, cloud computing has been receiving much attention as a new computing paradigm for providing flexible and on-demand infrastructures, platforms and software as services. Cloud computing has emerged as a result of combining the benefits of grid computing [58] with those of service-oriented computing [148] to utilize computer resources (*data centers*) and deliver computer resources as services. In the case of grid computing, computer hardware resources are combined from several organizations to achieve a certain goal (e.g., high performance and reduced costs), while in the case of service-oriented computing, computer software resources are designed and governed in the form of services. With cloud computing, computer resources are designed and governed in the form of services using virtualization techniques (e.g., the creation of virtual instances of the hardware platform, the operating system or the storage of network resources) to automate business logics since distributed systems are available for both public and private sectors. Cloud environments promise several benefits such as reduced expenses and simplicity to service providers and consumers [58, 138]. For instance, it only took 24 h, at the cost of merely $ 240, for the New York Times to archive its 11 million articles (1851–1980) using a cloud service named Amazon Web Services [64].

Given the accelerated adoption of cloud computing in the industry, trust management is still considered as one of the key challenges in the adoption of cloud computing. Indeed, according to the researchers at UC Berkeley [10], trust management and security are ranked among the top 10 obstacles for adopting cloud computing. This is because of challenging issues such as privacy [19, 30] (e.g., the leakage of Apple's iPad subscribers' information [101]), security [74, 145] (e.g., the mass email deletions of Gmail [11]), and dependability [73] (e.g., Amazon Web Services (AWS) outage that took down lots of business web sites [87]). In addition, the highly dynamic, distributed, and non-transparent nature of cloud services makes trust management even more challenging [10, 74, 103, 115].

An effective trust management service helps cloud service consumers and providers reap the benefits brought by cloud computing technologies. However, traditional trust management approaches such as the use of Service Level Agreement (SLA) are inadequate for complex cloud environments. SLAs alone are inadequate

© Springer International Publishing Switzerland 2014
T. H. Noor et al., *Trust Management in Cloud Services,*
DOI 10.1007/978-3-319-12250-2_1

to establish trust between cloud service consumers and providers because of its unclear and inconsistent clauses [67, 66]. For instance, in a recent survey [46], 46.6 % of consumers agree that SLA's legal contents are unclear. This makes the task of identifying trustworthy cloud services more difficult for cloud service consumers. Consumers' feedback is a good source to assess the overall trustworthiness of cloud services. Several researchers have recognized the significance of trust management and proposed solutions to assess and manage trust based on feedbacks collected from participants [26, 35, 66, 89, 106, 135].

This work focuses on tackling a number of research issues in credibility-based trust management of cloud services. Although the proposed techniques in our research are generic enough to be applicable to a wide range of applications, we use this motivating scenario as a running example throughout the book.

Figure 1.1 illustrates a trust management service which uses reputation to establish trust between cloud service consumers and providers. The top part of the figure shows different cloud service providers who provide one or several cloud services including Infrastructure as a Service (IaaS), Platform as a Service (PaaS), Software as a Service (SaaS) or a combination of them publicly available on the Internet. Cloud service providers are able to advertise their cloud services on the Internet. For example, some providers advertise their cloud services in search engines. The bottom part of the figure depicts different consumers who use cloud services. For example, a new startup that has limited funding can consume cloud services for hosting their services such as Amazon S3. A consumer can give trust feedbacks or inquire about the trust results of a particular cloud service by invoking the trust management service. The middle part of the figure depicts the trust management service which consists of several distributed nodes. These trust management service nodes expose interfaces so that consumers can give their feedback or inquire about the trust results in a decentralized way. The trust management service discovers cloud services through the Internet to allow consumers to search and assess the trust of new cloud services. The trust management service can advertise the trust as a service to consumers through the Internet.

This motivating scenario poses several major concerns including: (i) preserving the privacy of cloud service consumers since the interactions with the trust management service can involve sensitive information (Fig. 1.1, area 1); (ii) effective protection of cloud services by efficiently detecting malicious and amateur behaviors (Fig. 1.1, area 2); (iii) guaranteeing the availability of the trust management service due to the highly dynamic nature of cloud services (Fig. 1.1, area 3); (iv) automatic cloud services discovery to maintain an up-to-date cloud services repository to allow consumers to search and assess the trust of new cloud services (Fig. 1.1, area 4). Based on the observation in the aforementioned motivating scenario, credibility-based trust management of cloud services raises the following key issues:

- **Consumers' Privacy.** The adoption of cloud computing raises privacy concerns [115]. Consumers can have dynamic interactions with cloud service providers and the trust management service which involve sensitive information. There are several cases of privacy breaches such as leaks of sensitive information (e.g., date

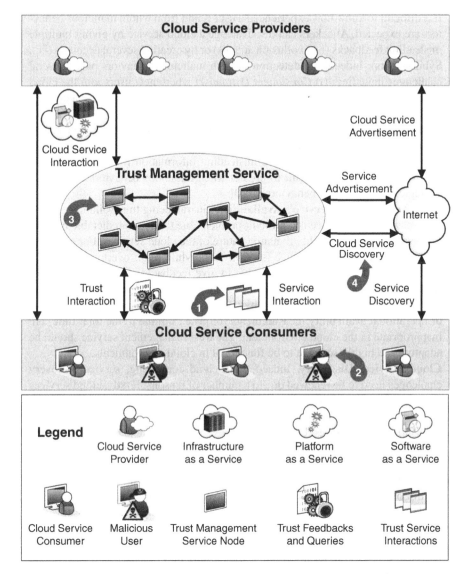

**Fig. 1.1** Motivating scenario

of birth and address) or behavioral information (e.g., with whom the consumer interacted, the kind of cloud services the consumer showed interest, etc.). Undoubtedly, services which involves consumers' data (e.g., interaction histories) should preserve the privacy [19].

- **Cloud Services Protection.** It is not unusual that the trust management service experiences attacks from its users. On the other hand, the quality of trust feedbacks differs from one person to another, depending on how experienced s/he is.

It is difficult to know how experienced a user is and from whom malicious behaviors are expected. Attackers can disadvantage a cloud service by giving multiple misleading feedbacks (i.e., collusion attacks) or by creating several accounts (i.e., Sybil attacks). Indeed, the detection of such malicious behaviors poses several challenges including: (i) *Consumers Dynamism* where new users join the cloud environment and old users leave around the clock which makes the detection of malicious behaviors (e.g., feedback collusion) a significant challenge, (ii) *Multiplicity of Identities* where users may have multiple accounts for a particular cloud service[1] which makes it difficult to detect Sybil attacks because malicious users can use multiple identities to give misleading information [59], (iii) *Attackers Behaviors* where it is difficult to predict when malicious behaviors occur (i.e., strategic VS. occasional behaviors) [120].

- **Trust Management Service's Availability.** Guaranteeing the availability of the trust management service is a difficult problem due to the unpredictable number of consumers and the highly dynamic nature of the cloud services. For example, if the trust management service is down for a while (e.g., overload or service update), then consumers will be unable to give feedbacks or inquire a trust assessment for cloud services. Consequently, approaches that require understanding of consumers' interests and capabilities through similarity measurements [134] or operational availability measurements [65] (i.e., uptime to the total time) are inappropriate in the cloud environment. The trust management service should be adaptive and highly scalable to be functional in cloud environments.

- **Cloud Services Discovery.** Indeed, with cloud computing, service discovery challenges need to be renewed due to a number of reasons. Firstly, cloud services are offered at different levels, not only providing data or business logic, but also infrastructure capabilities. Secondly, there lacks of standards for describing and publishing cloud services. Unlike Web services which use standard languages such as the Web Services Description Language (WSDL) or Unified Service Description Language (USDL) to expose their interfaces and the Universal Description, Discovery and Integration (UDDI) to publish their services to services' registries for discovery, the majority of the publicly available cloud services are not based on description standards [142, 148] which makes the cloud service discovery a challenging problem. For example, some publicly available cloud services do not mention "cloud" at all (such as `Dropbox` [51]). On the other hand, some businesses that have nothing to do with cloud computing (e.g., `cloud9carwash` [34]) may use cloud in their names or service descriptions.

In this book, we propose a framework for credibility-based trust management of cloud services. We also provide an implementation of our approach in the *Cloud Armor* (CLOud consUmers creDibility Assessment & tRust manageMent of clOud seRvices) prototype [109]. In Cloud Armor, the trust is delivered as a service where

---

[1] It is not uncommon nowadays that a user may have multiple accounts for a particular service such as owning multiple email accounts in Gmail.

the trust management service spans several distributed nodes to manage feedbacks in a decentralized way. Cloud Armor exploits crawling techniques for automatic cloud service discovery, credibility techniques for malicious behavior detection, and distributed techniques for high availability support. In a nutshell, the salient features of the proposed framework are:

- **Zero-Knowledge Credibility Proof Protocol.** Since that preserving the privacy is crucial for the adoption of cloud computing and the development of any services which involves consumers' data (i.e., consumers' identity attributes and interaction histories in our case), we introduce the *Zero-Knowledge Credibility Proof Protocol* (ZKC2P) [106, 107] that not only preserves the consumers' privacy, but also enables the trust management service to prove the credibility of a particular consumer's feedback. We propose that the Identity Management Service (IdM) can help the trust management service in measuring the credibility of trust feedbacks without breaching consumers' privacy. Anonymization techniques are exploited to protect consumers from privacy breaches in consumers' identities or interactions.
- **Robust and Adaptive Feedback Credibility Assessment.** The credibility of feedbacks plays an important role in the trust management service's performance. Therefore, we introduce a credibility model for robust and adaptive feedback credibility assessment. We propose several metrics for distinguishing between feedbacks from experienced and amateur consumers including *Consumer Capability* and *Majority Consensus* [103, 104].

  We further propose several metrics for the feedback collusion detection including the *Feedback Density* and *Occasional Feedback Collusion* [102, 105–107]. These metrics distinguish between misleading feedbacks from malicious users and credible ones from normal consumers. It also has the ability to detect strategic and occasional behaviors of collusion attacks (i.e., attackers who intend to manipulate the trust results by giving multiple trust feedbacks to a certain cloud service in a long or short period of time).

  In addition, we propose several metrics for the Sybil attacks detection including the *Multi-Identity Recognition* and *Occasional Sybil Attacks* [105–107]. These metrics allow the trust management service to identify misleading feedbacks from Sybil attacks (i.e., that occur strategically and occasionally). To adjust trust results for cloud services that have been affected by malicious behaviors, we introduce the metric of *Change Rate of Trust* [105, 106] that compensates the affected cloud services by the same percentage of damage.
- **Scalable and Distributed Service Nodes Management.** High availability is an important requirement to the trust management service. Thus, we introduce an availability model for scalable and distributed service nodes management. We propose to spread several distributed trust management service nodes to manage feedbacks given by consumers in a decentralized way. Load balancing techniques are exploited to share the workload, thereby always maintaining a desired availability level. The number of trust management service nodes is determined through an *operational power* metric that we introduce. In addition, replication techniques

are exploited to minimize the possibility of a node hosting a trust management service instance crashing which will allow it to recover any data lost during the down time from its replica. The number of replicas for each node is determined through a *replication determination* metric [102, 104] that we introduce. This metric exploits particle filtering techniques to precisely predict the availability of each node.

- **A Cloud Service Crawler Engine (CSCE).** We propose a *Cloud Service Crawler Engine* (CSCE) [108–110] that crawls search engines to collect cloud service information available on the Web. Our crawler engine has the capabilities to collect, validate, and categorize cloud services. By continuously crawling resources on the Web, it is possible to maintain an up-to-date cloud services repository for an effective and efficient cloud services discovery.

  To allow the crawler engine to collect, validate, and categorize cloud services, we develop the *Cloud Services Ontology* that facilitates the crawler engine with meta information and describes data semantics of cloud services, which is critical in the sense that cloud services may not necessarily use identifying words (e.g., cloud, infrastructure, platform and software) in their names and descriptions. When developing the cloud services ontology, we consider the cloud computing standard developed by NIST [96].

- **Datasets Collection.** Based on our observations, we believe that there is a need to identify, collect, and analyze cloud services currently available on the Web. This will help us to understand the current status of cloud services and gain valuable insights on future technical trends in the area. We used the cloud service crawler engine to do this task and the crawler managed to parse 619,474 possible links and discovered 35,601 possible seeds for cloud services. From the collected information, we prepare several large datasets of real-world cloud services and will release them to the research community. These datasets include nearly 6000 cloud services (1.06 GB) [108, 110].

- **Implementation and Performance Study.** We provide an implementation of our proposed credibility-based framework for trust management of cloud services in the *Cloud Armor* prototype [106, 108–110]. We develop a comprehensive platform for automatic cloud service discovery, malicious behavior detection, trust-based recommendation of cloud services and high availability support.

  To validate the feasibility and benefits of our approach, we conduct extensive experimental and performance studies of the proposed techniques using a collection of real-world trust feedbacks on cloud services. First, based on the collected data, we conduct a set of statistical analysis and present the results. These statistical results offer an overall view on the current status of cloud services. Second, we validate and study the performance of our credibility model by studying the effectiveness in distinguishing between feedbacks from experienced and amateur consumers, as well as studying the robustness of the proposed techniques against different malicious behaviors namely: collusion and Sybil attacks under several behaviors and performed several precision and recall measurements. Finally, we validate and study our availability model from various aspects including accuracy and performance.

Throughout the book, we will cover the details of the requirements, challenges, characteristics, and open research issues of deploying a credibility-based trust management approach for cloud services. Chapter 2 presents an overview of the cloud service models and trust management techniques. It surveys the representative research prototypes that efficiently support trust management of cloud services. It presents a generic analytical framework [111] that assesses existing trust management research prototypes in cloud computing and relevant areas using a set of assessment criteria. It also compares several major cloud service providers from a trust perspective.

Chapter 3 presents the overall view of the proposed credibility-based trust management framework. First, it provides details of the Zero-Knowledge Credibility Proof Protocol, and introduces the identify management service and the trust management service. It then discusses the assumptions and attack models.

Chapter 4 describes the details of the credibility model. It first introduces the consumer experience metrics, the feedback collusion detection metrics and the Sybil attacks detection metrics. It then describes the details of the feedback credibility aggregations and the metric of *Change Rate of Trust*.

Chapter 5 describes our Availability model. It first provides details of the proposed metrics including the *operational power* for sharing the workload of the trust management service nodes and the *replication determination* for minimizing the possibility of a node hosting a trust management service instance crashing. It then describes the proposed algorithms including *Particle Filtering based Algorithm*, *Trust Results and Credibility Weights Caching Algorithm* and *Instances Management Algorithm*.

Chapter 6 introduces the architecture design of the *Cloud Service Crawler Engine* (CSCE). It discusses the *Cloud Service Discovery Algorithm* and the cloud service ontology based on the cloud computing standard developed by NIST. It also discusses the design challenges of the crawler since the automatic discovery of cloud services is not a straightforward task.

Chapter 7 describes the implementation of the proposed approach for the credibility-based trust management of cloud services in the Cloud Armor prototype. It also reports the results for a set of statistical analysis on the collected datasets which offer an overall view on the current status of cloud services. It then reports the results of several experimental evaluations and performance studies for our credibility model and availability model. Finally, Chap. 8 provides concluding remarks of this book and discusses directions for future research.

# Chapter 2
# Background

An introduction to the research fields related to the trust management of services in cloud environments is given in this chapter to help readers gain a better understanding of the work described in this book. In particular, an overview of cloud services models and trust management techniques are presented in chapter. Furthermore, a generic framework is proposed to compare representative research prototypes and compare major cloud service providers [111].

This chapter is organized as follows. In Sects. 2.1 and 2.2, an overview of cloud services and their deployment models, and trust management techniques, are presented respectively. In Sect. 2.3, an analytical framework for trust management is proposed and a set of dimensions are identified for each layer in the framework to be used for comparing trust management solutions. In Sect. 2.4, 29 representative research prototypes are discussed and evaluated. In Sect. 2.5, several major cloud service providers are compared from a trust perspective. Finally, this chapter is summarized in Sect. 2.6.

## 2.1 Overview of Services in Cloud Environments

Cloud services are established based on five essential characteristics [96], namely, (i) *on-demand self-service* where cloud service consumers are able to automatically provision computing resources without the need for human interaction with each cloud service provider, (ii) *broad network access* where cloud service consumers can access available computing resources over the network, (iii) *resource pooling* where computing resources are pooled to serve multiple cloud service consumers based on a multi-tenant model where physical and virtual computing resources are dynamically reassigned on-demand, (iv) *rapid elasticity* where computing resources are elastically provisioned to scale rapidly based on the cloud service consumers need, and (v) *measured service* where computing resources usage is monitored, metered (i.e., using pay-as-you-go mechanism), controlled and reported to provide transparency for both cloud service providers and consumers. Based on the definition provided by the National Institute of Standards and Technology (NIST) [96], cloud computing can be defined as follows:

© Springer International Publishing Switzerland 2014      9
T. H. Noor et al., *Trust Management in Cloud Services,*
DOI 10.1007/978-3-319-12250-2_2

**Definition 2.1 (Cloud Computing)** *Cloud computing is a model for enabling ubiquitous, convenient, on-demand network access to a shared pool of configurable computing resources (e.g., networks, servers, storage, applications, and services) that can be rapidly provisioned and released with minimal management effort or service provider interaction. This cloud model is composed of five essential characteristics, three service models, and four deployment models.*  □

### 2.1.1  Cloud Service Models

Cloud services have three different models, including *Infrastructure as a Service* (IaaS), *Platform as a Service* (PaaS), and *Software as a Service* (SaaS) based on different Service Level Agreements (SLAs) between a cloud service provider and a consumer [26, 33, 96]. Figure 2.1 depicts the structured layers of cloud services:

*   *Infrastructure as a Service (IaaS).* This model represents the foundation part of the cloud environment where a cloud service consumer can rent the storage, the processing and the communication through virtual machines provided by a cloud service provider (e.g., Amazon's Elastic Compute Cloud (EC2) [6] and Simple Storage Service (S3) [7]). In this model, the cloud service provider controls and manages the underlying cloud environment, whereas the cloud service consumer has control over his/her virtual machine which includes the storage, the processing and can even select some network components for communication.
*   *Platform as a Service (PaaS).* This model represents the integration part of the cloud environment and resides above the IaaS layer to support system integration and virtualization middleware. The PaaS allows a cloud service consumer to develop his/her own software where the cloud service provider provisions the software development tools and programming languages (e.g., Google App [62]). In this model, the cloud service consumer has no control over the underlying cloud infrastructure (e.g., storage network, operating systems, etc.) but has control over the deployed applications.
*   *Software as a Service (SaaS).* This model represents the application part of the cloud environment and resides above the PaaS layer to support remote accessibility where cloud service consumers can remotely access their data which is stored in the underlying cloud infrastructure using applications provided by the cloud service provider (e.g., Google Docs [63], Windows Live Mesh [100]). Similarly, in this model, the cloud service consumer has no control over the underlying cloud infrastructure (e.g., storage network, operating systems, etc.) but has control over his/her data.

### 2.1.2  Cloud Service Deployment Models

Based on the Service Level Agreement (SLA), all cloud service models (i.e., IaaS, PaaS, SaaS) can be provisioned through four different cloud service deployment

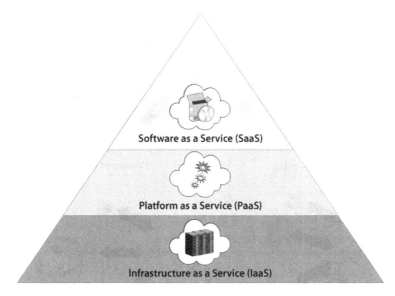

**Fig. 2.1** Cloud service models

models, namely *Private*, *Community*, *Public*, and *Hybrid* [96, 138] depending on the cloud service consumer's needs. Figure 2.2 depicts how cloud services are arranged to support these four cloud services deployment models and shows different interactions between cloud service providers and consumers. The interactions include Business-to-Business (B2B) and Business-to-Client (B2C).

- *Private Cloud.* In this deployment model, computing resources are provisioned for a particular organization (e.g., a business organization as shown in Fig. 2.2a), which involves several consumers (e.g., several business units). Essentially, interactions in this deployment model are considered as B2B interactions where the computing resources can be owned, governed, and operated by the same organization, a third party, or both.
- *Community Cloud.* In this deployment model, computing resources are provisioned for a community of organizations, as shown in Fig. 2.2b, to achieve a certain goal (e.g., high performance, security requirements, or reduced costs). Basically, interactions in this model are considered as B2B interactions where the computing resources can be owned, governed, and operated by the community (i.e., one or several organizations in the community), a third party, or both.
- *Public Cloud.* In this deployment model, computing resources are provisioned for the public (e.g., an individual cloud service consumer, academic, government, business organizations or a combination of these cloud service consumer types as shown in Fig. 2.2c). Essentially, interactions in this model are considered as B2C where the computing resources can be owned, governed, and operated by an academic, government, or business organization, or a combination of them.

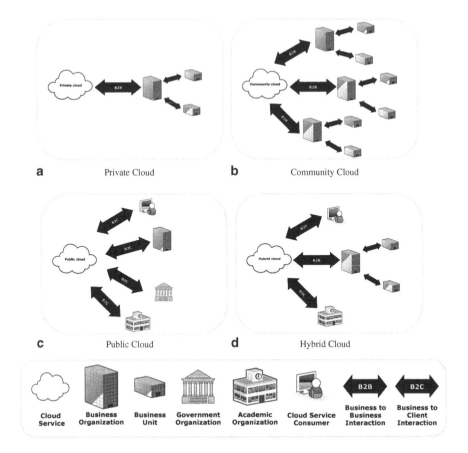

**Fig. 2.2**  Cloud service deployment models

- *Hybrid Cloud.* In this deployment model, computing resources are provisioned using two or more deployment models (e.g., private and public clouds can be deployed together using a hybrid deployment model as shown in Fig. 2.2b). Basically, interactions in this model include B2B and B2C interactions where computing resources are bound together by different clouds (e.g., private and public clouds) using portability techniques (e.g., data and application portability such as cloud bursting for load balancing between clouds).

Given all possible service and deployment models and interactions in cloud environments, we argue that there is no one trust management solution that fits all cloud services. A trust management service may be independent of cloud services but the trust techniques and assessment functions need to suit the underlying cloud service models. We believe that it is vital to know what are the possible trust management techniques and to identify which types of cloud services these techniques support well in order to give insights on how to develop the most suitable trust management solution for each type of cloud services. In the following section, we differentiate the trust management perspectives, classify the trust management techniques and present several examples for trust management systems in cloud environments.

## 2.2 Overview of Trust Management

Trust management is originally developed by Blaze et al. [22] to overcome the issues of centralized security systems, such as centralized control of trust relationships (i.e., global certifying authorities), inflexibility to support complex trust relationships in large-scale networks, and the heterogeneity of policy languages. Policy languages in trust management are responsible for setting authorization roles and implementing security policies. Authorization roles are satisfied through a set of security policies, which themselves are satisfied through a set of credentials. Some early attempts to implementing the trust management are PolicyMaker and KeyNote [21, 23–25]. These techniques are considered as policy-based trust management because they rely on policy roles to provide automated authorizations. Later, trust management inspired many researchers to specify the same concept in different environments such as e-commerce, Peer-to-Peer (P2P) systems, Web services, wireless sensor networks, grid computing, and most recently cloud computing. There are several trust definition reported in the literature from different perspectives. However, we agree with the one provided by Jøsang et al. [76]. So for this work we use the following definition:

**Definition 2.2 (Trust)** *Trust is the extent to which a cloud service consumer is willing to depend on a cloud service provider, provisioning a cloud service and expects certain qualities that the cloud service provider promised to be met.* □

Trust management is an effective approach to assess and establish *trusted relationships*. Several approaches have been proposed for managing and assessing trust based on different perspectives. We classify trust management using two different perspectives, namely: *Service Provider Perspective* (SPP) and *Service Requester Perspective* (SRP). In SPP, the service provider is the main driver of the trust management system where service requesters' trustworthiness is assessed (Fig. 2.3a). On the other hand, in SRP, the service requester is the one who assesses the trustworthiness of the service provider (Fig. 2.3b).

### 2.2.1 Trust Management Techniques

Different trust management techniques have been reported in the literature, which can be classified into four different categories: *Policy*, *Recommendation*, *Reputation*, and *Prediction*. To ease the discussion, we focus on explaining these trust management techniques using the service requester perspective (i.e., cloud service consumers perspective). The same techniques can be applied to the other perspective (i.e., cloud service providers perspective).

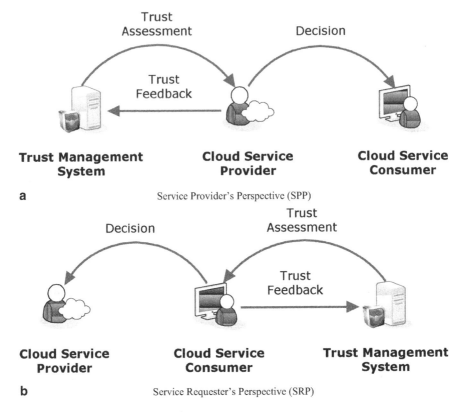

**Fig. 2.3** Trust management perspectives

Figure 2.4 depicts the four trust management techniques. Cloud service consumers and providers are connected with lines representing trusted relations between them (denoted $\mathcal{T}_r$). The values of $\mathcal{T}_r$ can be either 0 (the trusted relationship does not exist) or 1 (the trusted relationship exists). An unrecognized relation, denoted in a dashed line, occurs when a cloud service consumer $x$ approaches a cloud service provider $y$ for the first time.

### 2.2.1.1  Policy as a Trust Management Technique (PocT)

Policy as a trust management technique (PocT) is one of the most popular and traditional ways to establish trust among parties and has been used in cloud environments [4, 127, 154], the grid [136], P2P systems [137], Web applications [44] and the service-oriented environment [132, 133]. PocT uses a set of policies and each of which assumes several roles that control authorization levels and specifies a minimum trust threshold in order to authorize access. The trust thresholds are based on the trust results or the credentials.

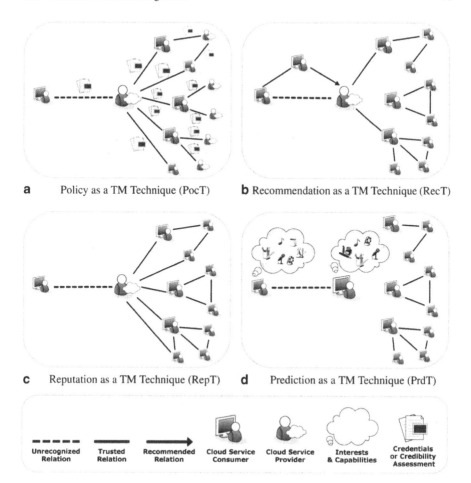

**Fig. 2.4** Trust Management (TM) techniques

For the trust results-based threshold, several approaches can be used. For instance, the *monitoring and auditing* approach proves Service Level Agreement (SLA) violations in cloud services (i.e., if the SLA is satisfied, then the cloud service is considered as trustworthy and *vise versa*). The *entities credibility* approach specifies a set of parameters to measure the credibility of parties [72] while the *feedback credibility* approach considers a set of factors to measure the credibility of feedbacks. SLA can be considered as a service plan (i.e., where the service level is specified) and as a service assurance where penalties can be assigned to the cloud service provider if there is a service level violation in the provisioned cloud services. SLA can establish trust between cloud service consumers and providers by specifying technical and functional descriptions with strict clauses. The entities credibility (i.e., the credibility of cloud services) can be measured from qualitative and quantitative attributes such as security, availability, response time, and customer support [67].

The feedback credibility [152] can be measured using several factors such as cloud service consumers' experience (i.e., the quality of feedbacks differs from one person to another [102]). Many researchers identify two features of credibility including trustworthiness and expertise [3, 89, 102, 140, 153].

For credential-based threshold, PocT follows either the Single-Sign-On (SSO) approach [114] where the credentials disclosure and authentication take place once and then the cloud service consumers have an access approval for several cloud services, or the state machine approach [143] where the credentials disclosure and authentication take place for each state of the execution of cloud services. Credentials are generally established based on standards such as the X.509v3 [36], the Simple Public Key Infrastructure (SPKI) [53], or the Security Assertion Markup Language (SAML) [29]. Many researchers use the digital certificates perspective to define the credential term [18, 28, 128] where a trusted third party (i.e., certificate authority) is required to certify the credential. However, not all credentials require a trusted certificate authority for establishing identities such as the Simple Public Key Infrastructure (SPKI) credentials [54] where the certificate authority is not required.

Figure 2.4a depicts how PocT is arranged to support trust management in the cloud environment. A cloud service consumer $x$ has certain policies $\mathcal{P}_x$ to control the disclosure of its own credentials $\mathcal{C}_x$ and contains the minimum trust threshold $\mathcal{T}_x$. $\mathcal{T}_x$ can either follow the credentials approach or the credibility approach, depending on the credibility assessment of the cloud service provider $y$ (denoted $\mathcal{R}_y$) to determine whether to proceed with the transaction. In contrast, the cloud service provider $y$ also has certain policies $\mathcal{P}_y$ to regulate access to its cloud services (e.g., IaaS, PaaS, SaaS), to control the disclosure of its own credentials $\mathcal{C}_y$ and contains the minimum trust threshold $\mathcal{T}_y$. Similarly, $\mathcal{T}_y$ can either follow the credential approach or the credibility approach, depending on the credibility assessment of the cloud service consumer $x$ (denoted $\mathcal{R}_x$). If both trust thresholds are satisfied (i.e., $\mathcal{T}_x$ and $\mathcal{T}_y$), the relation between the cloud service consumer $x$ and provider $y$ is considered as a trusted relation (i.e., $\mathcal{T}r(x, y) = 1$ as shown in Eq. 2.1).

$$\mathcal{T}r(x, y) = \begin{cases} 1 & if \quad \mathcal{C}_x \geq \mathcal{T}_y \Leftrightarrow \mathcal{C}_y \geq \mathcal{T}_x \ or \ \mathcal{R}_y \geq \mathcal{T}_x \Leftrightarrow \mathcal{R}_x \geq \mathcal{T}_y \\ 0 & otherwise \end{cases} \qquad (2.1)$$

The literature reports some efforts of PocT in cloud computing. For example, Brandic et al. [26] propose a novel language for specifying compliance requirements based on a model-driven technique and Ko et al. [80] present a TrustCloud framework that uses SLA detective controls and monitoring techniques for achieving trusted cloud services. Hwang et al. [73, 74] propose a security aware cloud architecture that uses pre-defined policies to evaluate the credibility of cloud services and Habib et al. [67] develop a multi-faceted Trust Management (TM) system to measure the credibility of cloud services based on Quality of Service (QoS) attributes such as security, latency, availability, and customer support. Finally, Noor and Sheng [102, 103] propose a credibility model that distinguishes credible feedbacks from the misleading ones. PocT is applicable for all three cloud service models.

### 2.2.1.2   Recommendation as a Trust Management Technique (RecT)

Recommendation as a trust management technique (RecT) has been widely used in the cloud environment [67, 82], the grid [49], and the service-oriented environment [113, 134]. Recommendations take advantage of participants knowledge about the trusted parties, especially given that the party at least knows the source of the trust feedback. It is well known in the social psychology theory that the role of a person has a considerable influence on another person's trust assessment if a recommendation is given [86]. Recommendations can appear in different forms such as the *explicit recommendation* or the *transitive recommendation*. An explicit recommendation happens when a cloud service consumer clearly recommends a certain cloud service to his/her well-established and trusted relations (e.g., friends). A transitive recommendation happens, on the other hand, when a cloud service consumer trusts a certain cloud service because at least one of his/her trusted relations trust the service.

Figure 2.4b depicts the RecT approach where the cloud service consumer $x$ has a trusted relation with another cloud service consumer $z$. Essentially, the cloud service consumer $z$ recommends consumer $x$ to cloud service provider $y$, or $x$ transitively trusts $y$ because there is a trusted relation between $z$ and $y$. In other words, because the cloud service consumer $x$ trusts the other cloud service consumer $z$, it is more likely that $x$ will trust the recommended relation (i.e., the cloud service provider $y$), $Tr(x, y \mid Tr(z, y)) = 1$ as shown in Eq. 2.2.

$$Tr(x, y \mid Tr(z, y)) = \begin{cases} 1 & if \quad Tr(z, y) = 1 \\ 0 & otherwise \end{cases} \tag{2.2}$$

One of the recent efforts using RecT in cloud computing is reported in [67]. In the work, trust is derived from recommendations using several operations including *consensus* (i.e., where trust feedbacks are aggregated from different cloud service consumers) and *discounting* (i.e., where trust feedbacks are weighted based on the trustworthiness of cloud service consumers). In [82], a cloud trust model is proposed based on transitive trust where a chain of trusted relations is built from a single root of trust. Similarly, RecT is applicable for all three cloud service models.

### 2.2.1.3   Reputation as a Trust Management Technique (RepT)

Reputation as a trust management technique (RepT) is important because the feedback of the various cloud service consumers can dramatically influence the reputation of a particular cloud service either positively or negatively. RepT has been used in the cloud environment [67, 82, 92, 102, 103], the grid [13–15, 85], P2P [8, 9, 41, 42, 77, 139, 140, 153, 158, 159], as well as the service-oriented environment [35, 89–91, 113]. Reputation can have direct or indirect influence on the trustworthiness of a particular entity (e.g., cloud service) as pointed in [3]. Unlike RecT, in RepT, cloud service consumers do not know the source of the trust feedback, i.e., there is no trusted relations in RepT, see Fig. 2.4b and 2.4c. There are several online reputation-based systems such as the auction systems (e.g., eBay [52] and Amazon [5]) where new and used goods are found, and the review systems [55] where the consumers opinions and reviews on specific products or services are expressed.

Figure 2.4c depicts how RepT supports trust management. The cloud service consumer $x$ has a certain minimum trust threshold $\mathcal{T}_x$ and the cloud service provider $y$ has a set of trusted relations $\mathcal{T}r(y) = \{r_1, r_2, \ldots, r_i\}$ (i.e., with other cloud service consumers), which give trust feedbacks on the cloud service provider $\mathcal{T}f(y) = \{f_1, f_2, \ldots, f_n\}$. These feedbacks are used to calculate the reputation of $y$, denoted as $\mathcal{R}ep(y)$, as shown in Eq. 2.3. The cloud service consumer $x$ determines whether to proceed with the transaction based on the reputation result of $y$. The more positive feedbacks that $y$ receives, the more likely $x$ will trust the cloud service provider $y$.

$$\mathcal{R}ep(y) = \frac{\sum_{x=1}^{|\mathcal{T}f(y)|} \mathcal{T}f(x, y)}{|\mathcal{T}f(y)|} \tag{2.3}$$

$$\mathcal{T}r\,(x,\,y) = \begin{cases} 1 & if \quad \mathcal{R}ep(y) \geq \mathcal{T}_x \\ 0 & otherwise \end{cases} \tag{2.4}$$

Similarly, there exist several efforts that use RepT in trust management of cloud computing. Habib et al. [67] focus on aggregating the reputation of a particular cloud service based on feedback using QoS and other attributes (e.g., elasticity, geographical location). The approach is applicable for different cloud service models. In [82], a reputation-based trust model is proposed that focuses on Infrastructure as a Service (IaaS) cloud services. Noor and Sheng [102, 103] propose a reputation-based trust management framework that distinguishes the credible feedbacks from the misleading ones.

### 2.2.1.4　Prediction as a Trust Management Technique (PrdT)

Prediction as a trust management technique (PrdT) is very useful especially when there is no prior information regarding the cloud service's interactions (e.g., previous interactions, history records) [134]. PrdT has been proposed in the cloud environment [67, 102, 103] and the service-oriented environment [134, 135]. The basic idea behind PrdT is that *similar minded entities* (e.g., cloud service consumers) are more likely to trust each other [94, 160].

Figure 2.4d depicts how PrdT works to support trust management. The cloud service consumer $x$ has some capabilities and interests (denoted $i_x$) represented in a vector space model by binary data, $i_x = (i_1, i_2, \ldots, i_j)$, and a certain minimum trust threshold $\mathcal{T}_x$ are used to determine whether to trust the other cloud service consumers. Similarly, the cloud service consumer $y$ also has some capabilities and interests (denoted as $i_y$) represented in a vector space model by binary data, $i_y = (i_1, i_2, \ldots, i_k)$, and a certain minimum trust threshold $\mathcal{T}_y$ is also used to determine

**Table 2.1** Notation and meanings in Chap. 2

| Notation | Meaning | Notation | Meaning |
|----------|---------|----------|---------|
| $\mathcal{T}_r$ | Trusted relationship. | $\mathcal{P}$ | Trust party's policies |
| $\mathcal{C}$ | Trust party's credentials | $\mathcal{T}$ | Trust party's minimum trust threshold |
| $\mathcal{R}$ | Trust party's credibility assessment | $\mathcal{T}f$ | Trust party's feedback |
| $\mathcal{R}ep$ | Trust party's reputation | $i$ | Trust party's capabilities and interests |
| $sim$ | The similarity measurement (e.g., the cosine similarity) | | |

whether to trust the other cloud service consumers. The similarity between those two vectors (i.e., $i_x$ and $i_y$) can be calculated using a similarity measurement such as the Cosine Similarity [134], as shown in Eq. 2.5. The more similar these capabilities and interests are, the more likely that the cloud service consumer $x$ will trust $y$.

$$sim\left(i_x, i_y\right) = \frac{i_x \cdot i_y}{\|i_x\| \cdot \|i_x\|} \tag{2.5}$$

$$\mathcal{T}r\left(x, y\right) = \begin{cases} 1 & if \quad sim\left(i_x, i_y\right) \geq \mathcal{T}_x \Leftrightarrow sim\left(i_x, i_y\right) \geq \mathcal{T}_y \\ 0 & otherwise \end{cases} \tag{2.6}$$

Noor and Sheng [102, 103] propose a similarity technique (i.e., distinguishing similar minded cloud service consumers) to determine credible feedbacks from the misleading ones. Habib et al. [67] uses PrdT to increase the quality of feedback where the trustworthiness of cloud service consumers is derived from the consensus of feedbacks (i.e., where feedbacks on a cloud service are similar to trust or distrust). PrdT can be used to refine the trust results and to increase the credibility of trust feedbacks. The notation and meanings in this chapter can be found in Table 2.1.

## 2.3 An Analytical Framework for Trust Management

In this section, we propose a generic analytical framework for trust management in cloud environments (see Fig. 2.5). In the framework, interactions in cloud applications occur at three layers. For each layer, a set of dimensions is identified that will be used as a benchmark to evaluate and analyze existing trust management research prototypes in Sect. 2.4.

### 2.3.1 Layers of the Trust Management Analytical Framework

The three layers of the trust management framework include: the *trust feedback sharing* layer, the *trust assessment* layer, and the *trust result distribution* layer (Fig. 2.5).

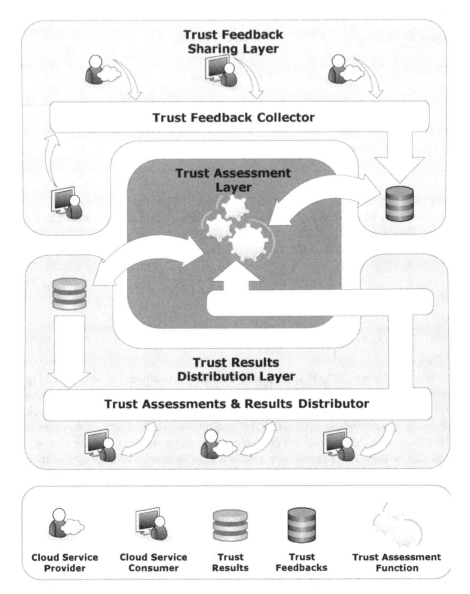

**Fig. 2.5** Architecture of the trust management analytical framework

• *Trust Feedback Sharing Layer (TFSL)*. TFSL consists of different parties including cloud service consumers and providers, which give trust feedbacks on each other. These feedbacks are maintained via a module called the Trust Feedback Collector. The feedbacks storage relies on the trust management systems, in the form of centralized, decentralized or even in the cloud environment through a trusted cloud service provider.

- *Trust Assessment Layer (TAL).* This layer represents the *core* of any trust management system: trust assessment. The assessment might contain more than one metric. TAL handles a huge amount of trust assessment queries from several parties through a module called the Trust Assessments and Results Distributor. This typically involves checking the trust results database and performing the assessment based on different trust management techniques (more details on trust management techniques can be found in Sect. 2.2.1). TAL delivers the trust results to a database in the trust results distribution layer through the module of the trust assessments and results distributor. This procedure is taken to avoid redundancy issues in trust assessment.
- *Trust Result Distribution Layer (TRDL).* Similar to TFSL, this layer consists of different parties including cloud service consumers and providers, which issue trust assessment inquiries about other parties (e.g., a cloud service consumer inquires about a specific cloud service). All trust assessment inquiries are transmitted to the trust assessment function through the module of trust assessments and results distributor. The final results are maintained in a database where cloud service consumers and providers can retrieve.

## 2.3.2  Dimensions for Evaluating Trust Management Research Prototypes

We identify a set of dimensions to study trust management issues where each layer of the framework has several dimensions. These dimensions are identified by considering the highly dynamic, distributed, and non-transparent nature of cloud environments.

### 2.3.2.1  The Trust Feedbacks Sharing Layer

There are four dimensions in this layer:

- *Credibility.* Credibility refers to the quality of the information or service that makes cloud service consumers or providers to trust the information or service. The credibility evaluation appears in several forms including the entity's credibility (e.g., a cloud service credibility) and the feedback credibility (more details are explained in Sect. 2.2.1.1). Since there is a strong relation between credibility and identification as emphasized in [43], the parallel data (i.e., feedback) processing require a proper identity scheme [147] for cloud service consumers and providers. For example, if no proper identity scheme is deployed, the trust management system can easily suffer from attacks such as *Sybil attacks* [59], which leads to low accuracy in trust results.
- *Privacy.* This dimension refers to the degree of sensitive information disclosure that the cloud service consumers might face during the interactions with the trust

management system. There are several cases of privacy breaches that may occur such as leaks of the cloud service consumers' sensitive information (e.g., user names, passwords, date of birth and address) or behavioral information (e.g., with whom the cloud service consumer interacted, the kind of cloud services the consumer showed interest, etc.). Indeed, cryptographic encryption techniques will decrease the data utilization [120] and traditional anonymization techniques (e.g., de-identification by removing personal identification information [60]) are inadequate in cloud environments [125] due to its highly dynamic and distributed nature.

• *Personalization.* Personalization refers to the degree of autonomy that the cloud service consumers and providers adhere to the trust management rules. Both can have proper personalization in their feedback designs and executions. This means that cloud service consumers and providers can select the feedback process (e.g., automated or manually driven) and the techniques they prefer. Personalization is applicable if the trust management system has fully autonomous collaboration, where each participant needs to interact via well-defined interfaces that allow participants to have control over their feedback and the flexibility to change their feedback processes without affecting each other. It is difficult to have a fully autonomous collaboration because of the complex translation features it requires [95].

• *Integration.* Integration refers to the ability to integrate different trust management perspectives and techniques. Participants can give their feedback from different perspectives (i.e., the cloud service provider and the cloud service consumer) through different trust management techniques (i.e., reputation, policy, etc.). Combining several trust management techniques can generally increase the accuracy of the trust results.

### 2.3.2.2  The Trust Assessment Layer

There are six dimensions in this layer:

• *Perspective.* Some trust management approaches focus on the cloud service provider's perspective while others focus on the cloud service consumer's perspective. It is therefore crucial to determine the perspective supported by a trust assessment function. The more perspectives the trust management system support, the more comprehensive the trust management system becomes.

• *Technique.* This dimension refers to the degree a technique can be adopted by the trust management system to manage and assess trust feedbacks. It is important to differentiate between the trust assessment functions that adopt a certain technique for trust management from the ones that adopt *several* trust management techniques together. Adopting several trust management techniques together can increase the accuracy of the trust results.

• *Adaptability.* Adaptability refers to how quickly the trust assessment function can adapt to changes of the inquisitive parties (i.e., cloud service providers or consumers). Some trust assessment inquiries can follow certain customized criteria from the inquisitive parties (e.g., weighing the feedback based on the size of the transaction), while others may follow the general trust assessment metric. In addition, updating feedbacks and trust results may be used as another indicator of adaptability because of the highly dynamic nature of cloud environments where new cloud service providers and consumers can join while others might leave at any time.

- *Security*. This dimension refers to the degree of robustness of the trust assessment function against malicious behaviors and attacks. There are two different security levels where attacks can occur: the *assessment function security level* and the *communication security level*. In the assessment function security level, there are several potential attacks against the trust assessment function including *whitewashing* [83], *self-promoting* [50], and *slandering* [16]. Self-promoting and slandering attacks can either occur in a *Non-collusive Malicious Behavior* (e.g., an attacker gives numerous misleading feedbacks in a short period of time to increase or decrease the trust results of a cloud service) or *Collusive Malicious Behavior* (e.g., several attackers collaborate to give numerous misleading feedbacks). At the communication security level, there are several attacks such as *Man-in-the-Middle* (MITM) attack [12] and *Denial-of-Service* (DoS) attack or distributed *Denial-of-Service* (DDoS) attack [71].
- *Scalability*. Given the highly dynamic and distributed nature of cloud environments, it is important that the trust management system be scalable. The scalability dimension refers to the ability of the trust management system to grow in one or more aspects (e.g., the volume of accessible trust results, the number of trust assessment inquiries that can be handled in a given period of time, and the number of trust relationships that can be supported). Trust models that follow a centralized architecture are more prone to several problems including scalability, availability and security (e.g., Denial-of-Service (DoS) attack) [70].
- *Applicability*. This dimension refers to the degree that the trust assessment function can be adopted to support trust management systems deployed for cloud services. It is important to differentiate the type of cloud services where the trust assessment functions are suitable. The more types of cloud services the trust assessment function can support, the more comprehensive the trust assessment function is.

### 2.3.2.3  The Trust Results Distribution Layer

There are four dimensions in this layer:

- *Response Time*. This is the time that the trust management system requires to handle trust assessment inquiries, to access feedbacks and to distribute trust results, especially when there is a significant number of trust relationships that are supported. If the trust management system needs a long response time, the number of inquiries that the trust management system will be able to handle will be low.
- *Redundancy*. This dimension refers to the degree of redundancy support that the trust management system maintains in order to manage and assess the trust feedbacks. There are two redundancy approaches: i) the *assessment redundancy* (i.e.,

the unnecessary process of duplication that the trust assessment function performs) which occur when multiple trust assessment inquiries are issued sequentially for the same cloud service, and ii) the *trust data redundancy* (i.e., the replication of the trust data including feedbacks and trust results) used to avoid scalability and monitoring issues. Redundancy causes resource waste and eventually affects the performance of the trust management system.

- *Accuracy.* Accuracy refers to the degree of correctness of the distributed trust results that can be determined through one or more accuracy characteristics such as the unique identification of feedbacks and using the proper assessment function security level. Poor identification of feedbacks can lead to inaccurate trust results while the lack of proper assessment security function makes the trust management system penetrable and the distributed trust results are more likely to be manipulated by attackers.
- *Security.* The security dimension refers to the degree of protection that the trust assessments and results distributor have against malicious behaviors and attacks. The *access control level* determines whether the trust management system uses any access control technique for the trust results distribution while security at the *communication level* is similar to that in the trust assessment layer. Ultimately, if the trust assessments and results distributor have higher protection against security threats, the trust management system becomes more reliable.

## 2.4  Research Prototypes

In this section, we present an overview of a set of representative research prototypes on trust management. These research prototypes are then analyzed and compared using the assessment dimensions identified in Sect. 2.3.2.

### 2.4.1  Overview of Major Research Prototypes

We present an overview of several representative trust management research prototypes on cloud computing and the most relevant areas such as the grid, Peer-to-Peer (P2P), and service-oriented computing.

- **Security-Aware Cloud Architecture:** In [73, 74], Hwang et al. propose a security-aware cloud architecture that uses Virtual Private Network (VPN) and Secure Socket Layer (SSL) for secure communication. The research focuses on different trust management perspectives such as the cloud service provider's and consumer's perspectives. From the service provider's perspective, the proposed architecture uses the trust negotiation and the data coloring (integration) approach based on the fuzzy logic technique and the Public-Key Infrastructure (PKI) for cloud service consumer authentication. From the service consumer's perspective, the proposed architecture uses the Distributed-Hash-Table (DHT)-based trust-overlay networks among several data centers to deploy a reputation-based trust management technique. Although it is mentioned that the architecture is reputation-based, it is actually based on pre-defined policies that evaluate the credibility of cloud services. In other words, the security aware cloud architecture is a policy-based trust management system because reputation is actually based on other trusted participants opinions (i.e., cloud service consumers feedbacks) on a specific cloud service (as described in Sect. 2.2.1).

- **Compliant Cloud Computing Architecture (C3):** Brandic et al. [26] propose a novel approach for compliance management in cloud environments to establish trust among different parties. The architecture focuses on cloud service consumer's perspective to protect cloud resources and preserve the privacy for all parties. This architecture is centralized and uses a certification mechanism for authentication, compliance management to help the cloud service consumers have proper choices in selecting cloud services. However, the architecture does not make use of other trust techniques such as *reputation, recommendation*, etc. which represent the participants' opinions. The authors further propose a novel language for specifying compliance requirements based on a model-driven technique using Unified Modeling Language (UML) for security, privacy and trust. The C3 middleware is responsible for the deployment of certifiable and auditable applications. This approach is considered to be a policy-based trust management system in the sense that it depends on policy compliance to enhance privacy, security and establish trust among cloud service providers and consumers.

- **TrustCloud: A Framework for Accountability and Trust in Cloud Computing:** Ko et al. [80] propose the TrustCloud framework for accountability and trust in cloud computing. The framework focuses on cloud service consumer's perspective to enforce cloud accountability and auditability. The framework exploits a centralized architecture, detective controls, and monitoring techniques for achieving trusted cloud services. In particular, TrustCloud consists of five layers, including *workflow, data, system, policies*, and *laws and regulations*, to address accountability in cloud environments. All these layers maintain the cloud accountability life cycle that consists of seven phases including *policy planning, sense and trace, logging, safe-keeping of logs, reporting and replaying, auditing,* and *optimizing and rectifying*.

- **Multi-faceted Trust Management System Architecture for Cloud Computing:** Habib et al. [67] propose a multi-faceted Trust Management (TM) system for cloud computing to help consumers identify trustworthy cloud service providers. The system focuses on the service consumer's perspective to establish trust relations between cloud service providers and consumers. It uses a centralized approach to collect trust-relevant information from multiple sources. In particular, the architecture models uncertainty of trust information using a set of Quality of Service (QoS) attributes such as security, latency, availability, and customer support. Finally, the architecture combines two different trust management techniques, namely reputation and recommendation.

- **Dynamic Policy Management Framework (DPMF):** Yu and Ng [156, 157] develop a dynamic policy management framework that allows authorization decisions for resource sharing among multiple virtual organizations to take place without requiring complete policy information. The framework focuses on the perspectives of both cloud service consumers and providers to protect organizations' resources and to preserve privacy for all trust entities. Similar to Cloud Armor, this framework has a decentralized architecture. The framework uses a *Conflict Analysis with Partial Information* (CAPI) mechanism to deploy a policy-based trust management system that measures similarities among policies to minimize policy disclosures.

- **Sabotage-Tolerance and Trust Management in Desktop Grid Computing:** In [49], Domingues et al. propose an approach for sabotage detection and a protocol for trust management that focuses on the service provider's perspective to protect grid resources and preserve privacy. This protocol has a centralized architecture that uses trust management based on a referral relationship technique (i.e., recommendation) for access control. Domingues et al. propose a *Volunteer Invitation-based System* (VIS) to deploy a recommendation-based trust management system that relies on the notion of responsibility clustering where each volunteer invitation holder has ultimate responsibility for referral relationships. These kinds of relationships are represented in a *trust tree* through multiple referral relationships where each level of the tree is responsible for the lower level's behavior.

- **Grid Secure Electronic Transaction (gSET):** Weishaupl et al. [149] develop a dynamic trust management framework for virtual organizations to minimize the credentials disclosure between different parties. The framework focuses on both the service provider's and the service requester's perspectives to protect virtual organizations' resources and privacy. This framework has a centralized architecture that uses PKI for authentication and trust management for access control. The authors adapt the *Secure Electronic Transaction* (SET) concept which is originally developed by MasterCard, Visa and others to suit the grid environment. The deployed framework is a policy-based trust management system that depends on PKI to enhance privacy, security and establish trust between service providers and requesters.

- **Role-Based Trust Chains:** In [31], Chen et al. present a heuristic-weighting approach to discover a specific set of credentials which is referred to as *credential chains* that satisfies several roles at control authorization levels. Instead of disclosing and authenticating credentials for each state of services such as state machines [143], the heuristic edge weighting approach allows the peer to choose the most likely path in credentials (i.e., credential chains) to minimize credential disclosures and establish role-based trust between peers in P2P networks. This approach has a decentralized architecture that uses a private key for authentication and credential chaining for role-based trust delegation. Credentials are signed by private keys to avoid their forgery. As a result, the deployed approach is considered as a policy-based trust management system that allows the service requesters to choose the most likely chain of credentials to establish trust delegation to access the resources that they select.

- **Bootstrapping and Prediction of Trust:** In [134], Skopik et al. propose a bootstrapping and prediction approach for trust management in large-scale systems.

The proposed techniques work when there is no prior information regarding a certain entity (e.g., no previous interactions, no history records, no external influence such as reputation, recommendations). The approach follows a centralized architecture and focuses on the service requester's perspective, helping them to choose the appropriate service. Skopik, et al. introduce the concepts of *mirroring* and *teleportation* of trust to deploy a trust management system that combines several trust management techniques such as *prediction* and *recommendation*. Both concepts depend on similarities among measures of interests and capabilities to establish trust between service requesters and providers. Although Skopik et al. claim that there is no prior information required regarding a certain entity, both concepts (i.e., mirroring and teleportation of trust) depend on previous, well-established and trustworthy relationships in order to measure the similarities in interests or capabilities. In the other words, it still presents a transitive trust flavor, representing an informal recommendation.

- **A Negotiation Scheme for Access Rights Establishment:** Koshutanski and Massacci [81] present a negotiation scheme that allows access rights establishment based on prior knowledge about the kind of credentials and privacy requirements that are needed to take the appropriate access decisions. The scheme focuses on the service provider's perspective, has a centralized architecture, and uses certificates for authentication. Koshutanski and Massacci develop a negotiation mechanism to deploy a policy-based trust management system that gives all parties prior notification about credentials and privacy requirements to minimize the credentials disclosure among parties. The framework does not have any particular mechanism or assumptions for secure communications.

- **A Trust Management Framework for Service-Oriented Environments (TMS):** Conner et al. [35] propose a trust management framework for Service-Oriented Architecture (SOA), which focuses on the service provider's perspective to protect resources from unauthorized access. This framework has a decentralized architecture that uses trust management for access control and it assumes secure communication. However, the framework does not have any particular mechanism for uniquely authenticating service requesters, which eventually leads to poor identification of trust feedbacks. The framework offers multiple trust evaluation metrics to allow trust participants to have their own customized evaluation. To reduce communication overheads, Conner et al. introduce a trust evaluation caching mechanism. This mechanism represents a good example for *assessment redundancy* (as described in Sect. 2.3.2.3) where the trust assessment function evaluates feedbacks only when necessary. The framework relies on a customized evaluation mechanism to deploy a reputation-based trust management system that allows service providers to assess their clients (i.e., service requesters) to establish trust between service providers and requesters. Although the framework allows customized trust evaluation, service providers need to develop their own reputation scoring functions.

- **Reputation Assessment for Trust Establishment Among Web Services (RATEWeb):** Malik and Bouguettaya [89–91] propose reputation assessment techniques based on QoS parameters. The techniques focus on the service requesters' perspective and the proposed system has a decentralized architecture where each service requester records his/her own perceptions of the reputation of a service provider. The proposed framework supports different models for feedback sharing including the *publish-subscribe collection* model, the *community broadcast collection* model, and the *credibility-based collection* model. Malik and Bouguettaya present several assessment metrics (e.g., rater credibility, majority rating, and temporal sensitivity), which enable the trust management system to combine several trust management techniques, such as *policy* and *reputation*, to improve the accuracy of trust results.

## *2.4.2  Evaluation of Trust Management Research Prototypes*

The evaluation of trust management prototypes covers 29 representative research prototypes where 69 % of these research prototypes have been published in the last 6 years and the rest represents some classical research prototypes that we cannot resist taking notice of them, due to their fundamental contribution and influence in the field of trust management. As shown in Fig. 2.6, the evaluation is organized to assess research prototypes using three different layers (i.e., the *trust feedback sharing* layer, the *trust assessment* layer and the *trust result distribution* layer) based on a set of dimensions, proposed in Sect. 2.3.

### 2.4.2.1  The Trust Feedback Sharing Layer (TFSL)

Figure 2.7a shows some statistical information of research prototypes on the TFSL layer. For the credibility dimension, we note that the majority of research prototypes (66 %) do not use any mechanisms to identify credible feedbacks in their trust models. For the privacy dimension, 52 % of research prototypes do not have any particular mechanism for preserving the privacy of parties; 45 % of research prototypes only focus on the service requesters' privacy and the rest 3 % focus on the privacy of both (i.e., service requesters and service providers). For the personalization dimension, a high proportion of research prototypes (76 %) does not consider the personalization aspect in their trust models and the rest research prototypes only use partial personalization in their trust models. Finally, for the integration dimension, the majority of research prototypes (72 %) do not make strong use of feedbacks combination.

### 2.4.2.2  Trust Assessment Layer (TAL)

Figure 2.7b depicts statistical information of research prototypes on the TAL layer. For the perspective dimension, we note that there is a fair degree of variety in the listed research prototypes. More than half of the research prototypes (55 %) focus on the service requester's perspective (SRP); 14 % of the research prototypes focus on the service provider's perspective (SPP); and the rest 31 % focus on both (i.e., SSP

| Prototypes | TFSL | | | | TAL | | | | | | TRDL | | | |
| | Credibility | Privacy | Personalization | Integration | Perspective | Technique | Adaptability | Security | Scalability | Applicability | Response Time | Redundancy | Accuracy | Security |
|---|---|---|---|---|---|---|---|---|---|---|---|---|---|---|
| Ko et al.11 | EC | SR | N | NFC | SRP | PocT[u] | N | AFL\CL | C | IaaS | NAT | N | F | ACL\CL |
| Habib, et al. 11 | EC | N | P | SFC | SRP | RecT\RepT\PrdT | P | AFL\CL | C | All | NAT | N | F | ACL\CL |
| Krautheim, et al. 10 | EC | SR | N | SFC | SRP\SPP | RecT\RepT | N | CL | C | IaaS | NAT | N | P | ACL\CL |
| Brandic et al. 10 | EC | SR | P | NFC | SRP | PocT[u] | P | CL | C | IaaS\PaaS | NAT | N | P | ACL\CL |
| Yao, et al. 10 | EC | N | N | NFC | SRP | PocT[u] | P | CL | C | IaaS | SAT | N | P | ACL\CL |
| Hwang, et al. 09 | EC | SR | N | NFC | SRP | PocT[rj] | N | AFL\CL | C | All | SAT | N | F | ACL\CL |
| Santos, et al. 09 | EC | SR | N | NFC | SRP | PocT | N | CL | D | IaaS | NAT | TR | P | ACL\CL |
| Manuel, et al. 09 | FC\EC | SR | N | SFC | SRP | PocT\RepT | N | AFL\CL | C | All | SAT | N | F | ACL\CL |
| Alhamad, et al. 10 | EC | SR | P | NFC | SRP | PocT[u]\RepT | N | N | D | IaaS | SAT | N | P | N |
| Azzedin and Maheswaran 02 | FC\EC | N | N | SFC | SRP | RepT | N | AFL | D | IaaS | SAT | AR\TR | P | ACL |
| Ching, et al. 04 | FC\EC | N | N | SFC | SRP\SPP | PocT\RepT | N | AFL\CL | D | IaaS | SAT | AR\TR | F | ACL\CL |
| Yu, et al. 06 | N | SR\SP | N | NFC | SRP\SPP | PocT | N | AFL | D | IaaS | NAT | AR\TR | P | ACL |
| Domingues, et al. 06 | EC[β] | N | N | NFC | SPP | RecT | N | N | C | All | NAT | N | N | ACL |
| Song, et al. 05a | EC | N | N | NFC | SRP | PocT[rj] | F | AFL\CL | C | IaaS | SAT | N | F | ACL\CL |
| Song, et al 05b | EC | N | N | NFC | SRP | PocT[rj] | F | AFL\CL | C | All | SAT | N | F | ACL\CL |
| Weishaupl, et al. 06 | N | SR | N | NFC | SRP\SPP | PocT | N | CL | C | IaaS | NAT | N | P | ACL\CL |
| Chen, et al. 08 | N | SR | P | NFC | SRP | PocT | N | AFL\CL | D | All | SAT | AR\TR | F | ACL\CL |
| Srivatsa, et al. 06 | FC\EC | N | N | NFC | SRP\SPP | RepT | F | AFL | D | All | SAT | TR | F | ACL |
| Aringhieri, et al. 06 | FC\EC | SR | N | NFC | SRP\SPP | RepT | P | AFL\CL | D | All | SAT | TR | F | ACL\CL |
| Zhou, et al. 07 | FC\EC | N | N | NFC | SRP\SPP | RepT | P | AFL\CL | D | All | SAT | TR | F | ACL\CL |
| Kamvar, et al. 03 | FC\EC | N | N | NFC | SRP\SPP | RepT | P | AFL | D | All | NAT | TR | N | ACL |
| Xiong, et al. 04 | FC\EC | N | N | NFC | SRP | RepT | F | AFL | D | All | NAT | AR\TR | P | ACL |
| Skopik, et al. 09 | N | N | N | SFC | SRP | RecT\PrdT | N | N | C | All | NAT | N | F | N |
| Skopik, et al. 10 | N | N | N | SFC | SRP | PocT\PrdT | N | CL | C | IaaS | SAT | TR | P | ACL\CL |
| Koshutanski, et al. 07 | N | SR | N | NFC | SPP | PocT | N | AFL | C | IaaS | NAT | N | F | ACL |
| Park, et al. 05 | FC\EC | N | N | SFC | SRP | RecT\RepT | N | AFL\CL | D | All | SAT | TR | F | ACL\CL |
| Skogsrud, et al. 04 | N | SR | P | NFC | SPP | PocT | F | AFL\CL | D | IaaS | SAT | TR | F | ACL\CL |
| Conner, et al. 09 | N | N | P | NFC | SPP | RepT | P | AFL | D | All | SAT | AR\TR | N | ACL |
| Malik, et al. 09 | FC\EC | SR | P | NFC | SRP | PocT\RepT | F | AFL | D | All | SAT | TR | F | ACL\CL |

Notes:

[rj] Although it is mentioned that the trust management system is based on *Reputation*, it is actually based on pre-defined policies that measure the credibility of the trust related parties (i.e., entities).

[β] Entity's credibility is identified through referral relationships.

[u] Service Level Agreement (SLA) is used to perform a *policy-based* trust management.

| Trust Feedbacks Sharing Layer (TFSL) | | | | | | |
|---|---|---|---|---|---|---|
| Credibility | | Privacy | | Personalization | Integration | |
| FC | Feedback Credibility | SP | Focus on Service Provider's Privacy | F | Full | SFC | Strong use of feedbacks combination |
| EC | Entity's Credibility | SR | Focus on Service Requester Privacy | P | Partial | NFC | No Strong use of feedbacks combination |
| N | None | N | None | N | None | | |

| Trust Assessment Layer (TAL) | | | | | |
|---|---|---|---|---|---|
| Perspective | Technique | Adaptability | Security | Scalability | Applicability |
| SPP Service Provider Perspective | PocT Policy Technique | F Full | AFL Support Assessment Function level | C Centralized | IaaS Infrastructure as a Service |
| SRP Service Requester Perspective | RecT Recommendation Technique | P Partial | CL Support Communication level | D Decentralized | PaaS Platform as a Service |
| | RepT Reputation Technique | N None | | | SaaS Software as a Service |

| Trust Results Distribution Layer (TRDL) | | | | |
|---|---|---|---|---|
| Response Time | Redundancy | Accuracy | Security | |
| SAT Strong Emphasis of Assessment Time | AR Support Assessment Redundancy | F Full | ACL Support Access Control level | |
| NAT No Strong Emphasis of Assessment Time | TR Support Trust Data Redundancy | P Partial | CL Support Communication level | |
| | N None | N None | N None | |

**Fig. 2.6** Evaluation of trust management research prototypes

and SRP). For the technique dimension, 41 % of research prototypes use policy as a trust management technique (PocT); 28 % of research prototypes use reputation as a trust management technique (RepT); 28 % of research prototypes use a combination of different trust management techniques (i.e., policy, recommendation, reputation, or prediction). Interestingly, only 3 % of research prototypes use recommendation as a trust management technique (RecT).

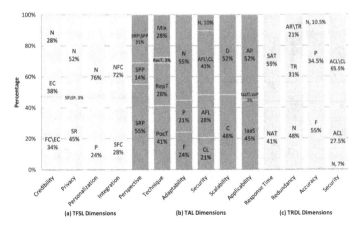

**Fig. 2.7** Statistical information of research prototypes evaluation

For the adaptability dimension, more than half of the representative research prototypes (55 %) do not support adaptability to changes that trusted parties require. 21 % of research prototypes support partial adaptability in their trust models and the remaining research prototypes (24 %) support full adaptability in their trust models. For the security dimension, 10 % of research prototypes do not use any security mechanisms; 21 % of research prototypes support secure communication; 28 % of research prototypes support the assessment function level security (AFL) and the rest (41 %) of research prototypes support both secure communication and AFL. For the scalability dimension, 52 % of research prototypes have a decentralized architecture for their trust management system. Finally, for the applicability dimension, 52 % of research prototypes can be adapted to support trust management system deployed for all types of cloud services (i.e., IaaS, PaaS, SaaS); 45 % of research prototypes use approaches suitable for IaaS cloud services. Only 3 % of research prototypes use approaches suitable for both models of IaaS and PaaS.

### 2.4.2.3  Trust Result Distribution Layer (TRDL)

Figure 2.7c shows the statistical information of the prototypes on the TRDL. For the response time dimension, we note that the majority of research prototypes (59 %) have a strong emphasis on the assessment time. For the redundancy dimension, 48 % of the research prototypes do not focus on redundancy techniques at all. 31 % of the research prototypes support trust results redundancy (TR) and the remaining prototypes (21 %) support both, i.e., TR and the trust assessment redundancy (AR). For the accuracy dimension, more than half of the representative research prototypes (55 %) are accurate in meeting the inquisitive parties expectations. 34.5 % of research prototypes have partial accuracy and 10.5 % have no accuracy in meeting the inquisitive parties expectations. Finally, for the security dimension, 7 % of research prototypes do not use any security mechanisms to mitigate potential attacks that target trust results. 27.5 % of research prototypes support the Access Control Level (ACL) security and the remaining prototypes (65.5 %) support the both (i.e, secure communication and ACL).

## 2.5   Cloud Service Providers

Major software vendors such as IBM, Microsoft, Amazon are offering different cloud services. The purpose of this section is to analyze these cloud services from the aspect of trust. It should be noted that there is a large number of cloud service providers and we will not be able to cover all of them. Instead, we focus on some major players in this arena. In this section, we first discuss a set of trust characteristics for cloud services and then compare several major cloud service providers.

### 2.5.1   Trust Characteristics in Cloud Services

Many researchers use a qualitative approach to compare existing cloud services for all three different service models (i.e., IaaS, PaaS and SaaS) among several cloud service providers from different perspectives such as the security features [73, 74], virtual infrastructure management capabilities [138], and services functionalities [27]. On the other hand, others use a quantitative approach to compare the use of cloud services among several cloud service providers (i.e., in terms of the number of cloud service consumers). For example, Guy Rosen has conducted a survey of the market use of the cloud computing [124]. The survey compares the number of publicly accessible websites hosted on several cloud services (about 500,000 sites). According to the survey [124], the number of sites (i.e., cloud service consumers) reached 3278 in August 2009 and this figure dramatically increased to nearly 9000 in January 2011. Intuitively, this is an indicator that the cloud environment is becoming increasingly attractive.

In the following, we define a set of trust characteristics, including *authentication*, *security*, *privacy responsibility*, *virtualization* and *cloud service consumer accessibility*, which will be used to compare several major cloud service providers:

- *Authentication.* This characteristic refers to the techniques and mechanisms that are used for authentication in a particular cloud. Cloud service consumers need to pay attention to the techniques that are used to establish their identities every time they attempt to use a new cloud service that indicates a certain extent on how trustworthy the cloud service is. To this end, consumers have to establish their identities every time they attempt to use a new cloud service by registering their credentials, which contain sensitive information. They can be subject to privacy breaches if no proper identity scheme is applied.

- *Security.* The security means that a cloud service uses can give a hint to consumers of the trustworthiness of this service. These means can be *Communication* Security Level (CSL), *Data* Security Level (DSL) and *Physical* Security Level (PSL). CSL refers to secure communication techniques such as Secure Socket Layers (SSL), DSL refers to data replication techniques for data recovery and PSL refers to physical security techniques such as hardware security.
- *Privacy Responsibility.* Knowing the privacy policy that a cloud service complies with can determine whether the consumer can trust his/her essential data out there somewhere (i.e., in the cloud datacenter). Based on SLAs the privacy responsibility can be split between providers and consumers. Provider's responsibility means that the cloud service assumes that the provider will deploy all the necessary security measures while consumer's responsibility means that the cloud service assume that the consumer will take all the necessary actions to preserve data privacy.
- *Virtualization.* The level of virtualization that a cloud service deploys can help consumers in determining what resources they have control over (e.g., storage) which indeed can be an indicator in identifying trustworthy cloud services. A cloud service has two levels of virtualization including *operating system* and *application container*. Virtualization techniques allow providers to control the underlying cloud environment, whereas consumers have control over their virtual machines which include storage and processes and some network components for communication.
- *Cloud Service Consumer Accessibility.* The type of accessibility that a cloud service offers can determine whether the consumer can reliably trust the cloud service or not. Consumers access cloud services using several means such as Graphical User Interfaces (GUIs), Application Programming Interfaces (APIs) and command-line tools.

### 2.5.2   Comparison of Major Cloud Service Providers

We compare several representative cloud service providers including IBM, Microsoft, Google and Amazon and the result is shown in Table 2.2. From the table we note that some of the cloud service providers (e.g., Amazon) focus on providing one cloud service model only while others (e.g., IBM and Microsoft) focus on providing all three service models (i.e., IaaS, PaaS and SaaS). It is worth mentioning that cloud service providers are targeting specific portions of cloud service consumers. For example, IBM is targeting only the service provider portion of the cloud service consumers. Consequently, most of the interactions are considered business-to-business interactions while other cloud service providers such as Microsoft, Google and Amazon are targeting both of the cloud service consumers portions (i.e., the service provider and service requesters). Thus, most of the interactions are Business-to-Business (B2B) and Business-to-Client (B2C).

**Table 2.2** Comparison: Representative Cloud Service Providers VS. Service Trust Characteristics

| Cloud service providers | IBM | | | Microsoft | | | Google | | Amazon |
|---|---|---|---|---|---|---|---|---|---|
| Supported service models | IaaS | PaaS | SaaS | IaaS | PaaS | SaaS PaaS | SaaS | IaaS | IaaS |
| Service types | Computation, storage | Web apps | Web apps | Storage | Web apps | Web apps | Web apps | Web apps | Computation, storage |
| Service names | Ensembles | BlueCloud, WebSphere CloudBurst Appliance, Research Compute Cloud (RC2) | Lotus Live | Microsoft Live Mesh | Windows Azure | .NET service, dynamic customer relationship management (CRM) | Google App Engine | Gmail, Google Docs | Elastic Compute Cloud (EC2), Simple Storage Service (S3), Simple Queue Service, SimpleDB |
| Authentication | Public-Key Infrastructure (PKI) and access management services | | | Rule-based access control, and password-based protection | | | Secure Shell (SSH) and Rule-based access control | | Password-based protection or Secure Shell (SSH)[a] |
| Communication security level | WebSphere2 (Secure Socket Layer (SSL)) or Virtual Private Network (VPN)[a] | | | Secure Socket Layer (SSL) for data transfers | | | Secure Socket Layer (SSL) for data transfers | | Secure Socket Layer (SSL) for data transfers |

**Table 2.2** (continued)

| Cloud service providers | IBM | Microsoft | Google | Amazon |
| --- | --- | --- | --- | --- |
| Data security level | Data de-duplication practices | Replicated data for data recovery | Grid-based redundancy | Elastic block store for failure recovery |
| Physical security level | Hardware security in data centers | Hardware security in data centers | Local and central monitoring techniques for Hardware security | Hardware security in data centers |
| Privacy | Cloud consumer's responsibility | Cloud Provider's responsibility | Cloud provider's responsibility | Cloud consumer's responsibility |
| Virtualization | Operating system level running on IBM PowerVM | Operating system level | Application container level | Operating system level running on a Xen hypervisor |
| Cloud service consumer accessibility | Browser-based accessible GUI using Dojo Toolkit | Web-based Live Desktop | Web-based Administration | Amazon EC2 Command-line Tools or API[a] |

[a] The cloud service consumer has the choice of provisioned technologies

Another interesting observation from Table 2.2 is that given the diverse number of available technologies, a cloud service consumer faces many configuration options when using cloud services. These options include the number of virtual machines, the type of virtual machines, time of tenancy, access control polices, etc. We argue that there is a need for intelligent techniques to make the cloud platform learn the patterns that cloud service consumers usually use to simplify the configuration process and make it more user-friendly. In addition, cloud service providers may deliver several cloud services that have similar features. It is very important for cloud service consumers to be able to choose a cloud service provider that provides *trustworthy* cloud services. The decision can be made on the basis of previous cloud service consumer's feedbacks where trust management is an effective approach to assess and establish trusted relationships.

## 2.6  Summary

In this chapter, we have introduced some basic concepts related to trust management of services in cloud environments and presented the state-of-the-art. In particular, we overviewed cloud services essential characteristics and their models. We then differentiated the trust management perspectives and classified trust management techniques into four categories. We proposed a generic framework that considers a holistic view of the issues related to the trust management for interactions in cloud environments. We also compared 29 representative trust management research prototypes in cloud computing and the relevant research areas using the proposed analytical framework. The framework consists of three layers and for each layer, we further identified a set of dimensions (i.e., assessment criteria), which are used as a benchmark, to study these research prototypes. Several major cloud service providers are also compared. In the next chapters, we will present the overall view of the proposed credibility-based trust management and discovery of cloud services framework.

# Chapter 3
# Trust Management and Discovery of Cloud Services

According to researchers at Berkeley et al. [10], trust and security are ranked as one of the top ten obstacles for the adoption of cloud computing. Service Level Agreements (SLAs) alone are inadequate to establish trust between cloud service consumers and providers because of its unclear and inconsistent clauses [66, 67]. For instance, in a recent survey [46], 46.6 % of consumers agree that SLA's legal contents are unclear. Consumers' feedback is a good source to assess the overall trustworthiness of cloud services. Several researchers have recognized the significance of trust management and proposed solutions to assess and manage trust based on feedbacks collected from participants [26, 35, 66, 89, 106, 135]. However, credibility-based trust management of cloud services raise privacy concerns because consumers can have dynamic inter-actions with cloud service providers and the trust management service which involve sensitive information. There are several cases of privacy breaches such as leaks of sensitive information (e.g., date of birth and address) or behavioral information (e.g., with whom the consumer interacted, the kind of cloud services the consumer showed interest, etc.). Undoubtedly, services which involves consumers' data (e.g., interaction histories) should preserve the privacy [19].

In this chapter, we describe our proposed framework for credibility-based trust management and discovery of cloud services which delivers Trust as a Service (TaaS). To preserve the privacy of consumers (i.e., by protecting consumers' sensitive infor-mation such as consumers' identity attributes and interaction histories), we introduce the *Zero-Knowledge Credibility Proof Protocol* (ZKC2P) [106, 107] that not only preserves the consumers' privacy, but also enables the trust management service to prove the credibility of a particular consumer's feedback.

This chapter is organized as follows. Section 3.1 gives an overview of the proposed trust management framework. The design of the Zero-Knowledge Credibility Proof Protocol, the details of the identity management service and the trust management service, as well as assumptions and attack models are described in Sect. 3.2. Finally, Sect. 3.3 reports the related work and Sect. 3.4 concludes this chapter.

© Springer International Publishing Switzerland 2014
T. H. Noor et al., *Trust Management in Cloud Services,*
DOI 10.1007/978-3-319-12250-2_3

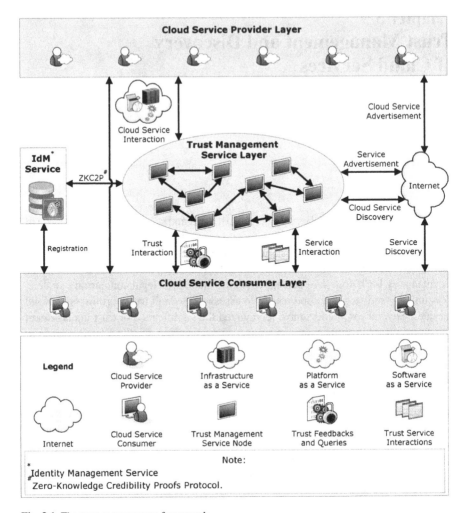

**Fig. 3.1** The trust management framework

## 3.1   Design Overview

We propose the trust management framework using the Service Oriented Architecture (SOA) to deliver trust as a service. SOA and Web services are one of the most important enabling technologies for cloud computing in the sense that resources (e.g., infrastructures, platforms, and software) are exposed in clouds as services [47, 148]. In particular, the trust management service spans several distributed nodes that expose interfaces so that consumers can give their feedbacks or inquire about the trust results. Figure 3.1 depicts the framework, which consists of three different layers, namely the *Cloud Service Provider Layer*, the *Trust Management Service Layer*, and the *Cloud Service Consumer Layer*.

- *The Cloud Service Provider Layer.* This layer consists of different cloud service providers who provide one or several cloud services (i.e., Infrastructure as a Service (IaaS), Platform as a Service (PaaS), and Software as a Service (SaaS)) publicly on the Web. These cloud services are accessible through web-portals and indexed on search engines such as Google, Yahoo, and Baidu. Interactions for this layer are considered as *Cloud Service Interaction* with consumers and the trust management service which is hosted in the cloud environment as well as *Cloud Services Advertisements* where providers are able to advertise their services on the Web (e.g., some cloud service providers advertise their cloud services in search engines).

- *The Trust Management Service Layer.* This layer consists of several distributed trust management service nodes which are hosted in several cloud environments allocated in different geographical areas. These trust management service nodes expose interfaces so that consumers can give their feedback or inquire about the trust results in a decentralized way. Interactions for this layer namely include: (i) *Cloud Service Interaction* with cloud service providers because the trust management service is hosted in the cloud environment, (ii) *Service Advertisement* to advertise the trust as a service to consumers through the *Internet*, (iii) *Cloud Service Discovery* through the *Internet* to allow consumers to assess the trust of new cloud services, (iv) *Trust* and *Service* interactions to allow consumers to give their feedbacks or inquire about the trust results, and (v) *Zero-Knowledge Credibility Proof Protocol* (ZKC2P) interactions to enable the trust management service to prove the credibility of a particular consumer's feedback (explained in detail in Sect. 3.2).

- The Cloud Service Consumer Layer. Finally, this layer consists of different consumers who use cloud services (i.e, IaaS, PaaS, or SaaS). For example, a new startup that has limited funding can consume cloud services (e.g., hosting their services in Amazon S3). A consumer can give trust feedbacks or inquire about the trust results of a particular cloud service by invoking the trust management service. Interactions for this layer namely include: (i) *Service Discovery* where consumers are able to discover new cloud services and other services through the *Internet*, (ii) *Trust* and *Service* interactions where consumers are able to give their feedback or inquire about the trust results of a particular cloud service, and (iii) *Registration* where consumers establish their identity through registering their credentials in the Identity Management service (IdM) before using the trust management service.

Our framework also exploits a web crawling approach for automatic cloud services discovery, where cloud services are automatically discovered on the Internet and stored in a *Cloud Services Repository*. Moreover, our framework contains an *Identity Management Service* (see Fig. 3.1) which is responsible for the *Registration* where consumers register their credentials before using the trust management service and proving the credibility of a particular consumer's feedback through the *Zero-Knowledge Credibility Proof Protocol* (ZKC2P).

## 3.2    The Zero-Knowledge Credibility Proof Protocol

Since there is a strong relation between trust and identification as emphasized in [43], we propose that the *Identity Management Service* (IdM) can help the *Trust Management Service* (TMS) in measuring the credibility of a consumer's feedback. However, processing the identity management service's information can breach the privacy of consumers. One way to preserve privacy is to use cryptographic encryption techniques but there is no efficient way to process encrypted data [115]. Another way is to use anonymization techniques to process the identity management service's information without breaching the privacy of consumers. However, there is clearly a trade-off between high anonymity and utility. On the one hand, full anonymization means better privacy. On the other hand, more utility means worse privacy (e.g., using a de-identification anonymization technique can still leak sensitive information through linking attacks [60]). Thus, we propose a *Zero-Knowledge Credibility Proof Protocol* (ZKC2P) to allow the trust management service to process the identity management service's information (i.e., credentials) using the *Multi-Identity Recognition* factor (explained in detail in Sect. 3.2). In other words, the trust management service will prove the consumers' feedback credibility without knowing the consumers' credentials. The trust management service processes credentials without including the sensitive information. Instead, anonymized information is used via consistent hashing (e.g., sha-256). The anonymization process covers all the credentials' attributes except the *Timestamps* attribute. The various credentials' attributes are explained in Sect. 3.2.1.

### 3.2.1    Identity Management Service (IdM)

Since trust and identification are closely related, as highlighted by David and Jaquet in [43], we believe that the identity management service can facilitate the trust management service in the detection of Sybil attacks against cloud services without breaching the privacy of consumers. When consumers attempt to use the trust management service for the first time, the trust management service requires them to register their credentials at the trust identity registry in the identity management service to establish their identities. The trust identity registry stores an identity record represented by a tuple $\mathcal{I} = (\mathcal{C}, \mathcal{C}_a, \mathcal{T}_i)$ for each consumer. $\mathcal{C}$ is the consumer's primary identity (e.g., user name). $\mathcal{C}_a$ represents a set of credentials' attributes (e.g., passwords, postal address, IP address, computer name, etc.) and $\mathcal{T}_i$ represents the consumer's registration time in the trust management service. More details on how the identity management service facilitates the trust management service in the detection of Sybil attacks can be found in Sect. 4.3.

### 3.2.2   Trust Management Service (TMS)

In a typical reputation-based trust management service, consumers either give feedback regarding the trustworthiness of a particular cloud service or request trust assessment for the service[1]. From consumers' feedback, the trust behavior of a cloud service is actually a collection of invocation history records, represented by a tuple $\mathcal{H} = (\mathcal{C}, \mathcal{S}, \mathcal{F}, \mathcal{T}_f)$, where $\mathcal{C}$ is the consumer's primary identity, $\mathcal{S}$ is the cloud service's identity, and $\mathcal{F}$ is a set of Quality of Service (QoS) feedbacks (i.e., the feedback represent several QoS parameters including availability, security, response time, accessibility, price, etc). Each trust feedback in $\mathcal{F}$ is represented in numerical form with the range of [0, 1], where 0, 1, and 0.5 means *negative*, *positive*, and *neutral* feedback respectively. $\mathcal{T}_f$ is the timestamps when the trust feedbacks are given. Whenever consumer $c$ requests a trust assessment for cloud service $s$, the trust management service calculates the trust result, denoted as $\mathcal{T}_r(s)$, from the collected trust feedbacks as follows:

$$\mathcal{T}_r(s) = \frac{\sum_{c=1}^{|\mathcal{V}(s)|} \mathcal{F}(c, s) * C_r\left(c, s, t_0, t\right)}{|\mathcal{V}(s)|} * (\chi * C_t(s, t_0, t)) \qquad (3.1)$$

where $\mathcal{V}(s)$ denotes the trust feedbacks given to cloud service $s$ and $|\mathcal{V}(s)|$ represents the total number of trust feedbacks. $\mathcal{F}(c, s)$ are trust feedbacks from the cth consumer weighted by the credibility aggregated weights $C_r(c, s, t_0, t)$ to allow the trust management service to dilute the influence of those misleading feedbacks from attacks. $\mathcal{F}(c, s)$ is held in the invocation history record $h$ and updated in the corresponding trust management service. $C_t(s, t_0, t)$ is the change rate of trust results in a period of time that allows the trust management service to adjust trust results for cloud services that have been affected by malicious behaviors. $\chi$ is the normalized weight factor for the change rate of trust results which increase the adaptability of the framework. More details on how to calculate $C_r(c, s, t_0, t)$ and $C_t(s, t_0, t)$ are described in Chap. 4.

### 3.2.3   Assumptions and Attack Models

In this book, we assume that the trust management service communications are secure because securing communications is not the focus of this work. Attacks such as *Man-in-the-Middle* (MITM) is therefore beyond the scope of this work. In this book, we consider the following types of attacks:

- **Collusion Attacks.** Also known as *collusive* malicious feedback behaviors, such attacks occur when several vicious users collaborate together to give numerous

---

[1] We assume a transaction-based feedback where all feedbacks are held in the trust management service.

misleading feedbacks to increase the trust result of cloud services (i.e., a self-promoting attack [50]) or to decrease the trust result of cloud services (i.e., a slandering attack [16]). This type of malicious behavior can occur in a *non-collusive* way where a particular malicious user gives multiple misleading feedbacks to conduct a self-promoting attack or a slandering attack.

- **Sybil Attacks.** Such an attack arises when malicious users exploits multiple identities [50, 59] to give numerous misleading feedbacks (e.g., producing numerous transactions by creating multiple virtual machines for a short period of time to leave fake feedbacks) for a self-promoting or slandering attack. It is interesting to note that attackers can also use multiple identities to disguise their negative historical trust records (i.e., whitewashing attacks [83]).

## 3.3  Related Work

Many research works have recognized the significance of trust management [70, 76, 111, 146]. In particular, trust management is considered as one of the critical issues in cloud computing and a very active research area [26, 74, 82, 92].

Several research works propose trust management techniques for cloud services. For instance, Habib et al. [67] proposed a multi-faceted Trust Management (TM) system architecture for cloud computing to help the cloud service consumers to identify trustworthy cloud service providers. In particular, the architecture models uncertainty of trust information collected from multiple sources using a set of Quality of Service (QoS) attributes such as security, latency, availability, and customer support. The architecture combines two different trust management techniques including reputation and recommendation where operators (e.g., AND, OR, NOT , FUSION, CONSENSUS, and DISCOUNTING) are used. Hwang et al. [74] proposed a security aware cloud architecture that assesses the trust for both the cloud service provider and consumers. To assess the trustworthiness of cloud service providers, Hwang et al. proposed the trust negotiation approach and the data coloring (integration) using fuzzy logic techniques. To assess the trustworthiness of cloud service consumers, they proposed the Distributed-Hash-Table (DHT)-based trust-overlay networks among several data centers to deploy a reputation-based trust management technique. Unlike previous works which did not consider the problem of unpredictable reputation attacks against cloud services, we present a credibility model (Chap. 4) that not only detects misleading feedbacks from collusion and Sybil attacks, but also has the ability to adaptively adjust trust results for cloud services that have been affected by malicious behaviors.

Some trust management approaches were proposed as policy-based trust management. For instance, Ko et al. [80] proposed TrustCloud framework for accountability and trust in cloud computing. In particular, TrustCloud consists of five layers including workflow, data, system, policies and laws, and regulations layers to address accountability in the cloud environment from all aspects. All of these layers maintain the cloud accountability life cycle which consists of seven phases including policy planning, sense and trace, logging, safe-keeping of logs, reporting and re-playing, auditing, and optimizing and rectifying. Brandic et al. [26] proposed a novel approach for compliance management in cloud environments to establish trust between different parties. The centralized architecture focuses on the cloud service consumer's perspective that uses compliant management to help consumers to have proper choices when selecting cloud services. Unlike previous works that usually use centralized architecture, we present a trust management framework support-ing distributed trust feedback assessment and storage. Moreover, previous works use policy-based trust management techniques, however, we evaluate the trustworthiness of a cloud service using reputation-based trust management techniques. Reputation represents a high influence that consumers have over the trust management sys-tem [45] especially that the opinions of the various consumers can dramatically influence the reputation of a cloud service either positively or negatively. We were inspired by Bertino et al. [19] in developing ZKC2P and the use of zero knowledge proofs but instead of using it for verification purposes, ZKC2P is used to measure the feedback credibility.

## 3.4 Summary

In this chapter, we have presented a framework for credibility-based trust manage-ment and discovery of cloud services which delivers Trust as a Service (TaaS) to allow consumers to effectively identify trustworthy cloud services. We introduce a *Zero-Knowledge Credibility Proof Protocol* (ZKC2P) that not only preserves the consumers' privacy, but also enables the trust management service to prove the cred-ibility of a particular consumer's feedback using an adaptive and robust *Credibility* model that will be explained in Chap. 4. The proposed framework relies on a decen-tralized architecture for trust management. It supports a scalable *Availability* model that dynamically decides the optimal number of the trust management service nodes to share the workload and always maintained at a desired availability level which will be explained in Chap. 5. Moreover, the framework provides a *Cloud Service Crawler Engine* for automatic cloud services discovery, explained in Chap. 6.

We have implemented the proposed trust management framework and also we conduct extensive experimental and performance studies of the proposed techniques using a collection of real-world trust feedbacks on cloud services. We will report the details of the implementation and experimental evaluation in Chap. 7.

# Chapter 4
# Robust and Adaptive Credibility Model

In reality, it is not unusual that a Trust Management Service (TMS) experiences malicious behaviors (e.g., collusion or Sybil attacks) from its users [66, 67, 89, 111]. Credibility-based trust management of cloud services poses cloud services protection issues because it is difficult to know how experienced a user is and from whom malicious behaviors are expected. On the one hand, the quality of trust feedbacks differs from one person to another, depending on how experienced s/he is. On the other hand, attackers can disadvantage a cloud service by giving multiple misleading feedbacks (i.e., collusion attacks) or by creating several accounts (i.e., Sybil attacks). Indeed, the detection of such malicious behaviors arises several challenges including: (i) *Consumers Dynamism* where new users join the cloud environment and old users leave around the clock which makes the detection of malicious behaviors (e.g., feedback collusion) a significant challenge, (ii) *Multiplicity of Identities* where users may have multiple accounts for a particular cloud service which makes it difficult to detect Sybil attacks because malicious users can use multiple identities to give misleading information [59], (iii) *Attackers Behaviors* where it is difficult to predict when malicious behaviors occur (i.e., strategic VS. occasional behaviors) [120].

In this chapter, we describe our proposed credibility model for robust and adaptive feedback credibility assessment to ensure the credibility of feedbacks given to the trust management service. We propose several metrics for distinguishing between feedbacks from experienced and amateur consumers (i.e., the *Consumer Experience*) including the *Consumer Capability* and *Majority Consensus* [103, 104]. We further propose several metrics for the *Feedback Collusion Detection* including the *Feedback Density* and *Occasional Feedback Collusion* [102, 105–107]. Moreover, we propose several metrics for the *Sybil Attacks Detection* including the *Multi-Identity Recognition* and *Occasional Sybil Attacks* [105–107]. To adjust trust results for cloud services that have been affected by malicious behaviors, we introduce the metric of *Change Rate of Trust* [105, 106] that compensate the affected cloud services by the same percentage of damage.

This chapter is organized as follows. Section 4.1 describes the consumer experience metrics including consumer capability and majority consensus. The details of the feedback collusion detection metrics including the feedback density and occasional feedback collusion are illustrated in Sect. 4.2. Section 4.3 reports the details

© Springer International Publishing Switzerland 2014
T. H. Noor et al., *Trust Management in Cloud Services,*
DOI 10.1007/978-3-319-12250-2_4

of the Sybil attacks detection metrics including the multi-identity recognition and occasional Sybil attacks. The details on the feedback credibility aggregations are described in Sect. 4.4. Section 4.5 describes the change rate of trust metric. Finally, Sect. 4.6 reports the related work and Sect. 4.7 concludes this chapter.

## 4.1   Consumer Experience

Sine the trust behavior of a cloud service in our framework is represented by a collection of invocation history records that contain cloud service consumers trust feedbacks (as mentioned in Chap. 3), the trust management service can receive *inaccurate* feedbacks from amateur cloud service consumers. To overcome this issue, in our *credibility model*, we consider the *consumer experience* where a consumer with considerable experience of giving trust feedbacks can gain a credibility as an *expert*. To be able to differentiate between expert and amateur consumers, we further consider several factors including the *Consumer Capability* and the *Majority Consensus*.

### 4.1.1   Consumer Capability

It is a common sense that older people are likely to be more experienced in judging things than younger people [123]. However, this is only true if the elder people have experienced considerable number of judging practices. As a result, we believe that "elder" cloud service consumers who have many judging practices are likely to be more experienced and capable than "younger" consumers with little experience. A consumer capability, denoted as $\mathcal{B}$, is measured as follows:

$$\mathcal{B}(c) = \begin{cases} 1 + \frac{|\mathcal{V}c(c)|}{\mathcal{A}g(c)} & if \quad |\mathcal{V}c(c)| \leq \mathcal{A}g(c) \\ 2 & otherwise \end{cases} \qquad (4.1)$$

where $\mathcal{V}c(c)$ represents all of the feedbacks given by consumer $c$ and $|\mathcal{V}c(c)|$ represents the length of $\mathcal{V}c(c)$ (i.e., the total number of feedbacks given by consumer $c$). $\mathcal{A}g(c)$ denotes the virtual *Age* of a certain consumer, measured in days since the registration in the trust management service. The idea behind adding the number 1 to this ratio is to increase the value of a consumer experience based on the capability result. In other words, we use $\mathcal{B}(c)$ as a *reward* factor. The higher the value of $\mathcal{B}(c)$ is, the more experienced a consumer is. It should be noted that even if a malicious consumer attempts to manipulate the capability result by giving numerous trust feedbacks in a short period of time, the capability result will not exceed 2.

## 4.1.2   Majority Consensus

It is well-known that the majority of people usually agree with experts' judgments about what is good [32]. Similarly, we believe that the majority of consumers agree with *Expert* consumers' judgments. In other words, any consumer whose trust feedback is close to the majority of trust feedbacks is considered an *Expert* consumer, *Amateur* consumer otherwise. In order to measure how close the consumer's trust feedbacks to the majority trust feedbacks (i.e., the *Majority Consensus*, $\mathcal{J}(c)$), we use the standard deviation (i.e., the root-mean-square) which is calculated as follows:

$$
\mathcal{J}(c) = 1 - \sqrt{\frac{\sum_{h \in \mathcal{V}c(c)} \left( \sum_{k=1}^{|\mathcal{V}c(c,\,k)|} \left( \frac{\mathcal{F}(c,\,k)}{|\mathcal{V}c(c,\,k)|} - \left( \frac{\sum_{l \neq c,l=1}^{|\mathcal{V}c(l,\,k)|} \mathcal{F}(l,\,k)}{|\mathcal{V}(k)| - |\mathcal{V}c(c,\,k)|} \right) \right) \right)^2}{|\mathcal{V}c(c)|}}
\tag{4.2}
$$

where the first part of the numerator represents the mean of consumer $c$'s trust feedbacks $\mathcal{F}(c, k)$ for the $k$th cloud service. The second part of the numerator represents the mean of the majority trust feedbacks given by other consumers denoted $\mathcal{F}(l, k)$ (i.e., the $l$th consumer trust feedbacks, except the consumer $c$'s trust feedbacks) to the $k$th cloud service. This procedure is done for all cloud services to which consumer $c$ give trust feedbacks (i.e., $\mathcal{V}c(c)$).

Based on the specified consumer's experience factors (i.e., consumer capability and majority consensus), the trust management service distinguishes between the *Expert* and *Amateur* consumers through assigning the *Consumer Experience* aggregated weights $Exp(c)$ to each of the cloud service consumers trust feedbacks as shown in Eqs. 4.10 and 3.1. The *Consumer Experience* aggregated weights $Exp(c)$ is calculated as follows:

$$
Exp(c) = \frac{\beta * \mathcal{B}(c) + \mu * \mathcal{J}(c)}{\lambda(Exp)}
\tag{4.3}
$$

where $\beta$ and $\mathcal{B}(c)$ denote the *Consumer Capability* factor's normalized weight (i.e., parameter) and the factor's value respectively. The second part of the equation represents the *Majority Consensus* factor where $\mu$ denotes the factor's normalized weight and $\mathcal{J}(c)$ denotes the factor's value. $\lambda(Exp)$ represents the number of factors used to calculate $Exp(c)$. For example, if we only consider consumer capability, $\lambda(Exp) = 1$; if we consider both, consumer capability and majority consensus, $\lambda(Exp) = 2$.

## 4.2   Feedback Collusion Detection

Attackers can disadvantage a cloud service by giving multiple misleading feedbacks (i.e., collusion attacks). Collusion attacks may occur strategically or occasionally which make it difficult to predict when such malicious behaviors may occur. To overcome this issue, in our *credibility model*, we consider several metrics for the feedback collusion detection including the *feedback density* and *occasional feedback collusion*.

### 4.2.1   Feedback Density

Some malicious consumers may give numerous fake feedbacks to manipulate trust results for cloud services (i.e., *Self-promoting* and *Slandering* attacks). Several on-line reputation-based systems such as eBay [52] have used the number of trusted feedbacks to help their consumers to overcome such attacks. The number of trusted feedbacks gives the evaluator a hint in determining the feedback credibility [153]. However, the number of trust feedbacks is not enough in determining the credibility of trust feedbacks. For instance, suppose there are two different cloud services $x$ and $y$ as shown in Fig. 4.1. The aggregated trust feedbacks of both cloud services are high (i.e., $x$ has 89 % positive feedbacks from 150 feedbacks, $y$ has 92 % posi-tive feedbacks from 150 feedbacks). Intuitively, consumers should proceed with the cloud service that has the highest aggregated trust feedbacks (e.g., $y$ in our case). However, a *Self-promoting* attack might have performed on cloud service $y$, which means $x$ should have been selected instead.

In order to overcome this problem, we introduce the concept of *Feedback Density* to support the determination of credible feedbacks. Specifically, we consider the total number of consumers who gave Feedback to a particular cloud service as the *Feedback Mass*, the total number of feedbacks given as the *Feedback Volume*. The feedback volume is influenced by the *Feedback Volume Collusion* factor which is controlled by a specified volume collusion threshold. This factor regulates the mul-tiple feedbacks extent that could collude the overall trusted feedback volume. For instance, if the volume collusion threshold is set to five feedbacks, any consumer $c$ who gives more than five feedbacks is considered to be suspicious of involving in a feedback volume collusion. The feedback density of a certain cloud service $s$, $\mathcal{D}(s)$, is calculated as follows:

$$\mathcal{D}(s) = \frac{\mathcal{M}(s)}{|\mathcal{V}(s)| * \mathcal{L}(s)} \tag{4.4}$$

where $\mathcal{M}(s)$ denotes the total number of consumers who gave feedbacks to cloud service $s$ (i.e., *Feedback Mass*). $|\mathcal{V}(s)|$ represents the total number of feedbacks given to cloud service $s$ (i.e., *Feedback Volume*). $\mathcal{L}(s)$ represents the *Feedback Volume Collusion* factor, calculated as follows:

$$\mathcal{L}(s) = 1 + \left( \frac{\sum_{h \in \mathcal{V}(s)} \left( \sum_{c=1}^{|\mathcal{V}_c(c,\,s)|} \left( \sum_{|\mathcal{V}_c(c,\,s)| > e_v(s)} |\mathcal{V}_c(c,\,s)| \right) \right)}{|\mathcal{V}(s)|} \right) \tag{4.5}$$

$\mathcal{L}(s)$ is calculated as the ratio of the number of feedbacks given by consumers $|\mathcal{V}_c(c, s)|$ who give feedbacks more than the specified volume collusion threshold

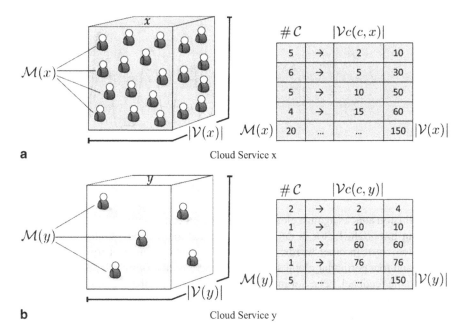

**Fig. 4.1** Trust feedback density determination

$e_v(s)$ over the total number of feedbacks received by the cloud service $|\mathcal{V}(s)|$. The idea is to reduce the value of the multiple feedbacks which are given diversely from the same consumer.

Figure 4.1 depicts the same example mentioned before where the first row in the table on the right side of Fig. 4.1a shows that five particular consumers gave two feedbacks to the cloud service $x$ in which the total number of those trust feedbacks is ten. The last row shows the total number of consumers (i.e., $\mathcal{M}(x) = 20$) and the total number of feedbacks given to the cloud service $x$ (i.e., $|\mathcal{V}(x)| = 150$). Both cloud services $x$ and $y$ have the same total number of feedbacks (i.e., $|\mathcal{V}(x)| = 150$ and $|\mathcal{V}(y)| = 150$) and very close aggregated feedbacks (e.g., $x$ has 89 % positive feedbacks and $y$ has 92 % positive feedbacks). However, the *Feedback Mass* of the cloud service $x$ is higher than the *Feedback Mass* of the cloud service $y$ (i.e., $\mathcal{M}(x) = 20$ and $\mathcal{M}(y) = 5$). If the volume collusion threshold $e_v$ is set to ten feedbacks per consumer, four consumers gave more than ten feedbacks to the cloud service $x$ (as shown in the fourth row in the table on the right side of Fig. 4.1a) where the total number of feedbacks $|\mathcal{V}_c(c, x)| = 60$; while two consumers gave more than ten feedbacks to the cloud service $y$ where the total number of feedbacks $|\mathcal{V}_c(c, y)| = 60 + 76 = 136$. According to Eq. 4.4, the *Feedback Density* of the cloud service $x$ is higher than the *Feedback Density* of the cloud service $y$ (i.e., $\mathcal{D}(x) = 0.0953$ and $\mathcal{D}(y) = 0.0175$). In other words, the higher the *Feedback Density*, the more credible the aggregated feedbacks are. The lower the *Feedback Density*, the more likely of a feedback collusion.

**Fig. 4.2** Occasional attacks
detection

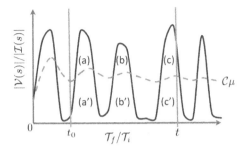

## 4.2.2   Occasional Feedback Collusion

Since collusion attacks against cloud services occur occasionally [120], we consider
*time* as an important factor in detecting occasional and periodic collusion attacks
(i.e., periodicity). In other words, we consider the total number of trust feedbacks
$|\mathcal{V}(s)|$ given to a particular cloud service $s$ during a period of time $[t_0, t]$. A sudden
change in the feedback behavior indicates an occasional feedback collusion because
the change of the number of feedbacks given to a cloud service happened abruptly
in a short period of time.

To detect such behavior, we measure the percentage of occasional change in the
total number of feedbacks among the whole feedback behavior (i.e., consumers'
behavior in giving feedbacks for a certain cloud service). The occasional feedback
collusion factor $\mathcal{O}_f(s, t_0, t)$ of cloud service $s$ in a period of time $[t_0, t]$, is calculated
as follows:

$$\mathcal{O}_f(s, t_0, t) = 1 - \left( \frac{\left( \int_{t_0}^{t} |\mathcal{V}(s,t)|\, dt \right) - \left( \int_{t_0}^{t} \Delta_f(s,t) dt \right)}{\int_{t_0}^{t} |\mathcal{V}(s,t)|\, dt} \right)$$

$$where \Delta_f(s,t) = \begin{cases} \mathcal{C}\mu\,(|\mathcal{V}(s,t)|) & if\ |\mathcal{V}(s,t)| \geq \\ & \mathcal{C}\mu\,(|\mathcal{V}(s,t)|) \\ |\mathcal{V}(s,t)| & otherwise \end{cases}$$

(4.6)

where the first part of the numerator represents the whole area under the curve
which represents the feedback behavior for the cloud service $s$ (i.e., $a \bigcup a'$, $b \bigcup b'$
and $c \bigcup c'$ in Fig. 4.2). The second part of the numerator represents the intersection
between the area under the curve and the area under the cumulative mean of the
total number of trust feedbacks $\mathcal{C}\mu\,(|\mathcal{V}(s,t)|)$ (i.e., the area $a' \bigcup b' \bigcup c'$ in Fig. 4.2).
$\mathcal{C}\mu\,(|\mathcal{V}(s,t)|)$ represents the mean of all points in the total number of trust feedbacks
and up to the last element because the mean is dynamic and changes from time to
time. The denominator represents the whole area under the curve. As a result, the
occasional collusion attacks detection is based on measuring the occasional change
in the total number of trust feedbacks in a period of time. The higher the occasional
change in the total number of trust feedbacks, the more likely that the cloud service
has been affected by an occasional collusion attack.

## 4.3 Sybil Attacks Detection

Malicious users can use multiple identities by creating several accounts and give misleading information to disadvantage a particular cloud service (i.e., Sybil attacks) which may occur strategically or occasionally. To overcome this issue, in our *credibility model*, we consider several metrics for the Sybil attacks detection including the *Multi-Identity Recognition* and *Occasional Sybil Attacks*.

### 4.3.1 Multi-identity Recognition

Since consumers have to register their credentials at the *Trust Identity Registry*, we believe that *Multi-Identity Recognition* is applicable by comparing consumers' credentials attributes values from the identity records $\mathcal{I}$. The main goal in this factor is to protect cloud services from malicious consumers who use multiple identities (i.e., *Sybil* attacks) to manipulate trust results. In a typical *Trust Identity Registry*, the entire identity records $\mathcal{I}$ are represented as a list of $m$ consumers' primary identities $C_p = \{p_1, p_2, ..., p_m\}$ (e.g., user name) and a list of $n$ credentials' attributes $C_a = \{a_1, a_2, ..., a_n\}$ (e.g., passwords, IP address, computer name, etc.). In other words, the entire $C_p \times C_a$ (Consumer's Primary Identity—Credentials' Attributes) Matrix, denoted as $IM$, covers all consumers who registered their credentials in the trust management services. The credential attribute value for a particular consumer $v_{c,t}$ is stored in the trust management service without including credentials with sensitive information using the ZKC2P (see Sect. 3.2).

We argue that the trust management service can identify patterns in consumers' anonymous credentials. Malicious users can use similar credentials in different identity records $\mathcal{I}$. Thus, we translate $IM$ to the *Multi-Identity Recognition Matrix*, denoted as $MIRM$, which similarly covers the entire identity records $\mathcal{I}$ represented as the entire $C_p \times C_a$. However, the value for a particular consumer $q_{c,t}$ in the new matrix represents the frequency of the credential attribute value for the same particular consumer $v_{c,t}$ in the same credential attribute (i.e., attribute $a_t$) as shown in Fig. 4.3. The frequency of a particular credential attribute value $v_{c,t}$, denoted as $q_{c,t}$, is calculated as the times of appearance (denoted as $\mathcal{A}_p$) that the credential value appears in the $t$th credential attribute normalized by the total number of identity records (i.e., the length of $a_t$) as follows:

$$q_{c,\,t} = \frac{\sum_{c=1}^{c=m} \left( \mathcal{A}_p(v_{c,\,t}) \right)}{|a_t|} \quad (4.7)$$

Then, the *Multi-Identity Recognition* factor $\mathcal{M}_{id}$ is calculated as the sum of frequencies of each credential attribute value for a particular consumer normalized by the total number of identity record as follows:

$$\mathcal{M}_{id}(c) = 1 - \left( \sum_{t=1}^{t=n} q_{c,\,t} \right) \quad (4.8)$$

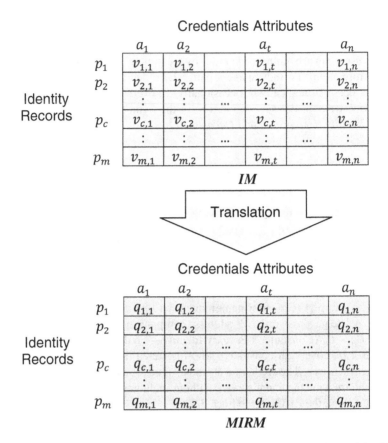

**Fig. 4.3** The Identity Records Matrix (IM) translation to the Multi-Identity Recognition Matrix (MIRM)

where the sum of $q_{c,t}$ represents the similar credentials distributed over different identity records $\mathcal{I}$ and $\mathcal{M}_{id}(c)$ represents the opposite (i.e., at least that the consumer has fairly unique credentials).

### 4.3.2  Occasional Sybil Attacks

Malicious users may manipulate trust results to disadvantage particular cloud services by creating multiple accounts and giving misleading feedbacks in a short period of time (i.e., Sybil attacks). To overcome the occasional Sybil attacks, we consider the total number of established identities $|\mathcal{I}(s)|$ for consumers who gave feedbacks to cloud service $s$ during a period of time $[t_0, t]$. The sudden changes in the total number of established identities is an indicator for an occasional Sybil attack. To detect such behavior, we measure the percentage of occasional and periodic change in the total number of established identities among the whole identity behavior (i.e., all established identities for consumers who gave feedbacks to a particular cloud service). Similarly, the occasional Sybil attacks factor $\mathcal{O}_i(s, t_0, t)$ of a certain cloud service $s$ in a period of time $[t_0, t]$, is calculated as follows:

$$\mathcal{O}_i(s, t_0, t) = 1 - \left( \frac{\left( \int_{t_0}^{t} |\mathcal{I}(s, t)| \, dt \right) - \left( \int_{t_0}^{t} \Delta_i(s, t) dt \right)}{\int_{t_0}^{t} |\mathcal{I}(s, t)| \, dt} \right)$$

$$where \, \Delta_i(s, t) = \begin{cases} \mathcal{C}\mu\left(|\mathcal{I}(s, t)|\right) & if \, |\mathcal{I}(s, t)| \geq \\ & \mathcal{C}\mu\left(|\mathcal{I}(s, t)|\right) \\ |\mathcal{I}(s, t)| & otherwise \end{cases} \tag{4.9}$$

where the first part of the numerator represents the whole area under the curve (i.e., the identity behavior for consumers who gave trust feedbacks to the cloud service $s$) as illustrated in Fig. 4.2. The second part of the numerator represents the intersection between the areas under the curve and the areas under the cumulative mean of the total number of established identities $\mathcal{C}\mu\left(|\mathcal{I}(s, t)|\right)$ (i.e., the area $a' \bigcup b' \bigcup c'$ in Fig. 4.2). The denominator represents the whole area under the curve (i.e., $a \bigcup a'$, $b \bigcup b'$ and $c \bigcup c'$ in Fig. 4.2). As a result, the occasional Sybil attacks detection is based on measuring the occasional and periodic change in the total number of established identities for consumers who gave trust feedbacks to a particular cloud service in a period of time. The higher the change in the total number of established identities, the more likely that the cloud service has been attacked by an occasional Sybil attack.

## 4.4 Feedback Credibility

Based on the proposed credibility metrics, the trust management service dilutes the influence of those misleading feedbacks by assigning the credibility aggregated weights $C_r(c, s, t_0, t)$ to each trust feedback as shown in Eq. 3.1 in Chap. 3. $C_r(c, s, t_0, t)$ is calculated as follows:

$$C_r(c, s, t_0, t) = \frac{Exp(c) + \rho * \mathcal{D}(s) + \phi * \mathcal{O}_f(s, t_0, t) + \Omega * \mathcal{M}_{id}(c) + \iota * \mathcal{O}_i(s, t_0, t)}{\lambda(C_r)}$$

$$\tag{4.10}$$

where $Exp(c)$ denote the *Consumer Experience* aggregated weights. $\rho$ and $\mathcal{D}(s)$ denote the *Feedback Density* factor's normalized weight (i.e., parameter) and the factor's value respectively. $\phi$ and $\mathcal{O}_f(s, t_0, t)$ denote the parameter of the occasional feedback collusion factor and the factor's value respectively. $\Omega$ denotes the *Multi-identity Recognition* normalized weight and $\mathcal{M}_{id}(c)$ denotes the factor's value. $\iota$

denotes the occasional Sybil attacks' normalized weight and $\mathcal{O}_i(s, t_0, t)$ denotes the factor's value. $\lambda(\mathcal{C}_r)$ represents the number of factors used to calculate $\mathcal{C}_r(c, s, t_0, t)$. For example, if we only consider feedback density, $\lambda(\mathcal{C}_r)$ will be 1; if we consider all credibility factors, $\lambda(\mathcal{C}_r)$ will be 5.

## 4.5   Change Rate of Trust Results

To allow the trust management service to adjust trust results for cloud services that have been affected by malicious behaviors, we introduce an additional factor on the change rate of trust results. The idea behind this factor is to compensate the affected cloud services by the same percentage of damage in the trust results. Given $Con(s, t_0)$ the conventional model (i.e., calculating the trust results without considering the proposed approach by calculating the mean of all feedbacks given to a particular cloud service) for cloud service $s$ in a previous time instance, $Con(s, t)$ the conventional model for the same cloud service calculated in a more recent time instance, the credibility aggregated weights $\mathcal{C}_r(c, s, t_0, t)$, and $e_t(s)$ the attacks percentage threshold. The change rate of trust results factor $\mathcal{C}_t(s, t_0, t)$ is calculated as follows:

$$\mathcal{C}_t(s, t_0, t) = \begin{cases} \left(\frac{Con(s, t_0)}{Con(s, t)}\right) + 1 & if \ Con(s, t) < Con(s, t_0) \\ & and \ 1 - \mathcal{C}_r(c, s, t_0, t) \geq e_t(s) \\ \\ 0 & otherwise \end{cases} \tag{4.11}$$

where $\left(\frac{Con(s, t_0)}{Con(s, t)}\right)$ represents the change rate of trust results for cloud service $s$ during a period of time $[t_0, t]$. The idea behind adding the number 1 to this ratio is to increase the trust result for the affected cloud services. The change rate of trust results will only be used if the conventional model in the more recent time instance is less than the conventional model in the previous time instance and the attacks percentage during the same period of time $[t_0, t]$ (i.e., $1 - \mathcal{C}_r(c, s, t_0, t)$) is larger or equal to the attacks percentage threshold. For instance, even if the conventional model in the current time for cloud service $a$ is less than the conventional model 10 days ago, cloud service $a$ will not be rewarded because the attacks percentage is less than the attacks percentage threshold (e.g., $1 - \mathcal{C}_r(c, a, t_0, t) = 20\%$ and $e_t(a) = 30\%$). The change rate of trust results is designed to limit the rewards to cloud services that are affected by slandering attacks (i.e., cloud services that have decreased trust results) because the trust management service can dilute the increased trust results from self-promoting attacks using the credibility factors (i.e., $\mathcal{C}_r(c, a, t_0, t)$). The adaptive change rate of trust results factor can be used to assign different weights using $\chi$ the normalized weight factor as shown in Eq. 3.1 in Chap. 3. The notation and meanings in this chapter can be found in Table 4.1.

**Table 4.1** Notation and meanings in Chap. 4

| Notation | Meaning | Notation | Meaning |
|---|---|---|---|
| $\mathcal{T}_r(s)$ | The trust result for cloud service $s$ | $\mathcal{F}$ | The consumer feedback for a curtain cloud service |
| $|\mathcal{V}(s)|$ | The total number of trust feedbacks given to cloud service $s$ (i.e., feedback volume) | $C_r(c, s, t_0, t)$ | The credibility aggregated weights |
| $C_t(s, t_0, t)$ | The change rate of trust results for cloud service $s$ in a period of time $[t_0, t]$ | $\chi$ | The normalized weight factor for the change rate of trust results |
| $\mathcal{B}(c)$ | Capability for consumer $c$ | $|\mathcal{V}c(c)|$ | The total number of trust feedbacks given by consumer $c$ |
| $\mathcal{A}g(c)$ | The virtual $Age\ of\ consumer\ c$ | $\mathcal{J}(c)$ | The majority consensus for consumer $c$ |
| $Exp(c)$ | Experience for consumer $c$ | $\beta$ | The consumer capability factor's parameter |
| $\mu$ | The majority consensus factor's parameter | $\lambda$ | The number of metrics used to calculate a particular factor (e.g., $Exp(c)$) |
| $\mathcal{D}(s)$ | The feedback density for cloud service $s$ | $\mathcal{M}(s)$ | The feedback mass for cloud service $s$ |
| $\mathcal{L}(s)$ | The feedback volume collusion factor for cloud service $s$ | $e_v$ | The volume collusion threshold |
| $\mathcal{O}_f(s, t_0, t)$ | The occasional feedback collusion factor of cloud service $s$ in a period of time $[t_0, t]$ | $C\mu$ | The cumulative mean in a period of time (e.g., the cumulative mean of the total number of trust feedbacks or established identities) |
| $v_{c,t}$ | The credential attribute anonymized value | $q_{c,t}$ | The frequency of a particular credential attribute value $v_{c,t}$ |
| $\mathcal{A}_p$ | The times of appearance of a credential value | $|a_t|$ | The total number of identity records |
| $\mathcal{M}_{id}(c)$ | The multi-identity recognition for consumer $c$ | $\mathcal{O}_i(s, t_0, t)$ | The occasional Sybil attacks factor of cloud service $s$ in a period of time $[t_0, t]$ |
| $\rho$ | The feedback density factor's parameter | $\phi$ | The occasional feedback collusion factor's parameter |
| $\Omega$ | The multi-identity recognition factor's parameter | $\iota$ | The occasional Sybil attacks factor's parameter |
| $Con$ | The conventional model | $e_t(s)$ | The attacks percentage threshold of cloud service $s$ |

## 4.6   Related Work

Several trust management approaches were proposed as reputation-based trust management. For example, Conner et al. [35] proposed a trust management framework for the Service-Oriented Architecture (SOA) that focuses on the service provider's perspective to protect resources from unauthorized access. This framework has a decentralized architecture that offers multiple trust evaluation metrics to allow service providers to have customized evaluation to assess their clients. Malik and Bouguettaya [90] proposed reputation assessment techniques based on the existing Quality of Service (QoS) parameters. The proposed framework supports different assessment metrics such as majority rating, past rating history, personal experience for credibility evaluation, etc. Unlike previous works that require extensive computations or trust participants' collaboration by rating the trust feedbacks, we present a robust and adaptive credibility model that include several metrics which facilitates the determination of credible trust feedbacks. We were inspired by Xiong and Liu who differentiate between the credibility of a peer and the credibility of a feedback through distinguishing several parameters to measure the credibility of the trust participants feedbacks [153]. However, their approach is not applicable in cloud environments because peers give and receive services and they are evaluated on that base. In other words, trust results are used to distinguish between credible and malicious feedbacks.

A few research works focused on the protection from malicious behaviors. For instance, Srivatsa and Xiong [139] proposed a reputation-based trust management; namely TrustGuard framework for peer-to-peer distributed environment. The framework uses several techniques to protect the trust management system from malicious peers such as a cost model that makes regaining reputation for malicious peers more difficult, unforgeable transaction proofs using time stamps and personalized similarity measurement for increasing the accuracy of the trust results. Other approaches were proposed such as Entropy-Based screening to drop the unfair trust feedbacks [150], filtering to waive out the unfair trust feedbacks, and majority rating scheme (i.e., centroid rating clustering), as well as, trust feedback rating to assign proper weights for trust feedbacks [89]. Unlike previous works, our credibility model not only detects misleading feedbacks from collusion attacks but also detects misleading feedbacks from Sybil attacks and has the ability to adaptively adjust trust results for cloud services that have been affected by malicious behaviors.

## 4.7   Summary

In this chapter, we have presented novel techniques that help in detecting reputation attacks to allow consumers to effectively identify trustworthy cloud services. We introduce a robust and adaptive credibility model that not only identifies misleading trust feedbacks from collusion attacks but also detects Sybil attacks no matter these attacks take place in a long or short period of time (i.e., strategic or occasional attacks respectively). To distinguish between feedbacks from experienced and amateur consumers, we propose several metrics including *Consumer Capability* and *Majority Consensus*. We further propose several metrics for the feedback collusion detection including the *Feedback Density* and *Occasional Feedback Collusion*. In addition, we propose several metrics for the Sybil attacks detection including the *Multi-Identity Recognition* and *Occasional Sybil Attacks*. To adjust trust results for cloud services that have been affected by malicious behaviors, we introduce the metric of *Change Rate of Trust*.

We have implemented the proposed credibility model and also we conduct extensive experimental and performance studies of the proposed techniques using a collection of real-world trust feedbacks on cloud services. We will report the details of the implementation and experimental evaluation in Chap. 7.

# Chapter 5
# Scalable Availability Model

Guaranteeing the availability of the trust management service is a difficult problem due to the unpredictable number of cloud service consumers and the highly dynamic nature of the cloud services. For example, if the trust management service is down for a while (e.g., overload or service update), the cloud service consumers will be unable to give feedbacks or inquire a trust assessment for cloud services. Consequently, approaches that require understanding of consumers' interests and capabilities through similarity measurements [134] or operational availability measurements [65] (i.e., uptime to the total time) are inappropriate in the cloud environment. The trust management service should be adaptive and highly scalable to be functional in cloud environments.

In this chapter, we describe our proposed availability model for scalable and distributed service nodes management, since high availability is an important requirement to the trust management service. We propose to spread several distributed trust management service nodes to manage feedbacks given by consumers in a decentralized way as mentioned in Sect. 3. Load balancing techniques are exploited to share the workload, thereby always maintaining a desired availability level. The number of trust management service nodes is determined through an *operational power* metric proposed in our work. In addition, replication techniques are exploited to minimize the crash possibility of a node hosting a trust management service instance which will allow it to recover any data lost during the down time from its replica. The number of replicas for each node is determined through a *replication determination* metric [102, 104]. This metric exploits particle filtering techniques to precisely predict the availability of each node. We further describe the proposed algorithms including *Particle Filtering based Algorithm*, *Trust Results and Credibility Weights Caching Algorithm* and *Instances Management Algorithm*.

This chapter is organized as follows. Section 5.1 describes the operational power metric for the number of trust management service nodes determination. The details of the replication determination metric and the particle filtering based algorithm are introduced in Sect. 5.2. Section 5.3 reports the details of the trust results and credibility weights caching algorithm. The details on the instances management algorithm are described in Sect. 5.4. Finally, Sect. 5.5 overviews the related work and Sect. 5.6 concludes this chapter.

© Springer International Publishing Switzerland 2014

T. H. Noor et al., *Trust Management in Cloud Services,*

DOI 10.1007/978-3-319-12250-2_5

## 5.1 Operational Power

In our approach, we propose to spread the trust management service nodes over various clouds and dynamically direct requests to the appropriate trust management service node (e.g., with lower workload), so that its desired availability level can be always maintained. It is crucial to develop a mechanism that helps determine the optimal number of trust management service nodes $\mathcal{N}$ because more nodes residing at various clouds means higher overhead (e.g., cost and resource consumption such as bandwidth and storage space) while lower nodes means less availability. To exploit the load balancing technique, we propose that each node hosting a trust management service instance reports its operational power. The operational power factor compares the workload for a particular trust management service node with the average workload of all trust management service nodes. The operational power for a particular trust management service node, $\mathcal{O}_p(s_{tms})$, is calculated as the mean of the *Euclidean distance* (i.e., to measure the distance between a particular trust management service node workload and the mean of the workload of all trust management service nodes) and the trust management service node workload (i.e., the percentage of trust feedbacks handled by this node) as follows:

$$\mathcal{O}_p(s_{tms}) = \frac{\left( \sqrt{\left( \frac{\mathcal{V}(s_{tms})}{\mathcal{V}(all_{tms})} - \frac{\mathcal{V}(mean_{tms})}{\mathcal{V}(all_{tms})} \right)^2} + \frac{\mathcal{V}(s_{tms})}{\mathcal{V}(all_{tms})} \right)}{2} \tag{5.1}$$

where the first part of the equation represents the *Euclidean distance* between the workload of node $s_{tms}$ and the average workload of all nodes where $\mathcal{V}(mean_{tms})$ denotes the mean of feedbacks handled by all nodes. The second part of the equation represents the ratio of feedbacks handled by a particular node $\mathcal{V}(s_{tms})$ over the total number of feedbacks handled by all nodes $\mathcal{V}(all_{tms})$. This ratio helps us to identify whether the workload of a particular node has triggered the workload threshold $e_w(s_{tms})$ or not; because the *Euclidean distance* alone is not enough. For example, suppose there are two different nodes $x_{tms}$ and $y_{tms}$ where the *Euclidean distance* for both nodes is equal to 10. The average workload of all nodes is equal to 50 and $e_w(s_{tms}) = 60$. However, $y_{tms}$ is the only node that triggers $e_w(s_{tms})$ because the ratio of feedbacks handled by $y_{tms}$ is equal to 60 while the ratio of feedbacks handled by $x_{tms}$ is equal to 40.

Based on the operational power factor, the trust management service uses $e_w(s_{tms})$ to automatically adjust the number of nodes $\mathcal{N}_{tms}$ that host the trust management service instances by creating extra instances to maintain a desired workload for each trust management service node. The number of nodes $\mathcal{N}_{tms}$ is adjusted as follows:

$$\mathcal{N}_{tms} = \begin{cases} \mathcal{N}_{tms} + 1 & if \quad \mathcal{O}_p(s_{tms}) \geq e_w(s_{tms}) \\ & or \quad \mathcal{N}_{tms} < 1 \\ \mathcal{N}_{tms} & otherwise \end{cases} \tag{5.2}$$

## 5.2 Replication Determination

In our trust management framework, we propose to exploit replication techniques to minimize the possibility of a node hosting a trust management service instance crashing as aforementioned in Chap. 3. The trust management service instance can crash for several reasons such as overload, service repair, service update, etc. which makes consumers unable to give trust feedbacks or request a trust assessment for cloud services. Replication will allow the trust management service instance to recover any data lost during the down time from its replica. In particular, we propose a particle filtering approach to precisely predict the availability of each node hosting a trust management service instance which then will be used to determine the optimal number of replicas for each instance. To predict the availability of each node, we model the trust management service instance as an instantaneous (or point) availability.

To predict the availability of each node, we firstly adopt the point availability to model the trust management service instance's availability, then use the particle filtering technique to estimate the availability. We model the probability of the trust management service instance as the point availability [20], which denotes the functional probability at a specific time $t$. It can be denoted as:

$$A(s_{tms}, t) = 1 - F(t) + \int_0^t m(x)(1 - F(t - x))dx \qquad (5.3)$$

where $1 - F(x)$ is the probability of no failure in $(0, t]$, $m(x)dx$ is denoting the probability that no failure occurs in any one of the renewal points in interval $(x, x + dx]$, and $1 - F(t - x)$ is the probability that no further failure occurs in $(x, t]$. So this availability function is a function of time parameter and can be estimated for different points of time. This equation can be solved by Laplace transform, rewritten as:

$$A(s_{tms}, t) = \frac{1 - f(t)}{t(1 - f(t)g(t))} \qquad (5.4)$$

where $f(t)$ and $g(t)$ are the Laplace transforms of the failure-free and renewal density function. In our work, failure free density follows the exponential distribution and renewal density function follows the Poisson distribution.

So we can model the trust management service instance's availability prediction problem via defining the state function and measurement function respectively as below:

$$z(t + 1) = A(s_{tms}, t) + \epsilon_z$$
$$y(t + 1) = z(t + 1) + \epsilon_y \qquad (5.5)$$
$$where \quad \epsilon_z \sim \mathcal{N}(0, \sigma_z^2), \epsilon_y \sim \mathcal{N}(0, \sigma_y^2)$$

Secondly, we use the particle filtering technique to estimate and track the availability. A particle filter is a probabilistic approximation algorithm implementing a Bayes

---

**Algorithm**: Particle Filtering based Algorithm

---

1. **Initialization:** compute the weight distribution $\mathcal{D}_w(\mathcal{A}(s_{tms}))$ according to prior knowledge on replicas, e.g., the IP address of server hosting replicas etc.

2. **Generation:** generate the particle set and assign the particle set containing $\mathcal{N}$ particles

- generate initial particle set $\mathcal{P}_0$ which has $\mathcal{N}$ particles, $\mathcal{P}_0 = (p_{0,0}, p_{0,1}, ...p_{0,\mathcal{N}-1})$ and distribute them in a uniform distribution in the initial stage. Particle $p_{0,k} = (\mathcal{A}(s_{tms})_{0,k}, weight_{0,k})$
- assign weight to the particles according to our weight distribution $\mathcal{D}_w(\mathcal{A}(s_{tms}))$.

3. **Resampling:**

- Resample $\mathcal{N}$ particles from the particle set from a particle set $\mathcal{P}_t$ using weights of each particles.
- generate new particle set $\mathcal{P}_{t+1}$ and assign weight according to $\mathcal{D}_w(\mathcal{A}(s_{tms}))$

4. **Estimation:** predict new availability of the particle set $\mathcal{P}_t$ based on availability function $\mathcal{A}(s_{tms}, t)$.

5. **Update:**

- recalculate the weight of $\mathcal{P}_t$ based on measurement $m$, $w_{t,k}=$ $\prod(\mathcal{D}_w(\mathcal{A}(s_{tms})_{t,k}))(\frac{1}{\sqrt{2\pi}\sigma_y})exp(-\frac{\delta\mathcal{A}(s_{tms})_{t,k}^2}{2\sigma_y^2})$, where $\delta\mathcal{A}(s_{tms})_k = m_\mathcal{A}(s_{tms}) - \mathcal{A}(s_{tms})_{t,k}$
- calculate current availability by mean value of $p_t(\mathcal{A}(s_{tms})_t)$

6. Go to step 3 and iteration until convergence

---

**Fig. 5.1** Particle filtering based algorithm

filter and a sequential Monte Carlo method, for the availability estimation in our work. It maintains a probability distribution for the estimated availability at time $t$, representing the belief of the trust management service instance's availability.

We initialize a uniformly distributed sample set representing the trust management service instance's availability state. We assign each sample a same weight $w$. When the availability changes, the particle filter will calculate the measurement by adjusting and normalizing each sample's weight. These samples' weights are proportional to the observation likelihood $p(y|z)$. The particle filters randomly draw samples from the current sample set whose probability can be given by the weights. Then we can apply the particle filters to estimate the possible next availability state for each new particle. The prediction and update steps will keep going until convergence.

We calculate the weight distribution by considering the bias resulted from the routing information between users and targeting trust management service node (e.g., routing-hops between the user and the trust management service node or whether user and targeting node are in the same IP address segment). The Sequential Importance Sampling (SIS) algorithm consists of recursive propagation of the weights and support points as each measurement is received sequentially. To tackle the degeneracy problem, we adopt a more advanced algorithm with resampling [93]. It has less time complexity and minimizes the Monte-Carlo variation. The overall particle filtering based estimation methodology is summarized in Fig. 5.1.

Based on the predicted availability of the trust management service instance $\mathcal{A}(s_{tms}, t)$, let $e_a$ denote the availability threshold (ranging from 0 to 1), and $r$ be the

**Fig. 5.2** Trust management
service replication number
determination

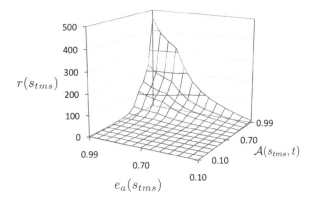

total number of $s_{tms}$ replicas, the desired goal of the replication is to ensure that at
least one replica is available, represented in the following formula:

$$e_a\left(s_{tms}\right) < A\left(s_{tms}, t\right)^{r\left(s_{tms}\right)} \tag{5.6}$$

where $A\left(s_{tms}, t\right)^{r\left(s_{tms}\right)}$ represents the probability of at least one trust management
service instance's replica is available. As a result, the optimal number of trust
management service instance's replicas can be calculated as follows:

$$r\left(s_{tms}\right) > log_{A\left(s_{tms}, t\right)}\left(e_a(s_{tms})\right) \tag{5.7}$$

For example, if the availability threshold $e_a\left(s_{tms}\right) = 0.99$ and the predicted availability of the trust management service instance $A\left(s_{tms}, t\right) = 0.2$ (low), $r\left(s_{tms}\right) > 2.86$,
meaning that at least 3 trust management service instance's replicas are needed.
Similarly, if $e_a\left(s_{tms}\right) = 0.99$ and the predicted availability of the trust management
service instance $A\left(s_{tms}, t\right) = 0.8$ (high), $r\left(s_{tms}\right) > 20.64$ which means at least 21
replicas are required. Figure 5.2 depicts the relationship between the main compo-
nents of the replication determination. It can be clearly seen that the relationship
between $A\left(s_{tms}, t\right)$ and $r\left(s_{tms}\right)$ is a direct or positive relationship (i.e., any change in
$A\left(s_{tms}, t\right)$ is associated with a change in $r\left(s_{tms}\right)$).

## 5.3  Trust Result Caching

Due to the credibility factors that we proposed in Chap. 4 when computing the
trust result for a particular cloud service, it would be odd if the trust management
service instance retrieves all trust feedbacks given to a particular cloud service and
computes the trust result every time it receives a trust assessment request from a user.
Instead we propose to cache the trust results and the credibility weights based on the
number of new trust feedbacks to avoid unnecessary trust result computations. The

---

**Algorithm**: Trust Results & Credibility Weights Caching Algorithm
**Input**: $s$ /*Cloud Service ID*/
**Output**: $\mathcal{T}r(s)$ /*The Trust Result for Cloud Service $s$*/

---

Count $|\mathcal{V}c(c, s)|_{Cache}$ /*TMS instance counts the total number of new trust feedbacks given by a particular consumer*/
**if** $|\mathcal{V}c(c, s)|_{Cache} \geq e_{Cache}(c)$ **then** /*TMS determines whether a recalculation is required for credibility factors related to the consumer*/
        Compute $\mathcal{J}(c)$
        Compute $\mathcal{B}(c)$
        Compute $\mathcal{M}_{id}(c)$
        Compute $\mathcal{C}r(c, s)$
**end if**
Count $|\mathcal{V}(s)|_{Cache}$ /*TMS instance counts the total number of new trust feedbacks given to a particular cloud service*/
**if** $|\mathcal{V}(s)|_{Cache} \geq e_{Cache}(s)$ **then** /*TMS determines whether a recalculation is required for credibility factors related to the cloud service including the trust result*/
        Compute $\mathcal{D}(s)$
        Compute $\mathcal{C}r(c^{\varsigma} s)$
        Compute $\mathcal{T}r(s)$
**end if**

---

**Fig. 5.3** Trust results & credibility weights caching algorithm

caching process is controlled by two thresholds, one for consumers $e_{Cache}(c)$ and one for cloud services $e_{Cache}(s)$. If the trust management service instance receives a trust assessment request from a user it uses the trust result in the cache instead of computing the trust result. The trust management service instance will update the cache based on the number of new trust feedbacks (i.e., since the last update) given by a particular consumer $|\mathcal{V}c(c, s)|_{Cache}$ and the number of new trust feedbacks given to a particular cloud service $|\mathcal{V}(s)|_{Cache}$. The caching process is briefly shown in the Algorithm in Fig. 5.3. The notation and meanings in this chapter can be found in Table 5.1.

## 5.4  Instances Management

In our trust management framework, we propose that the trust management service instance $tms_{id}(0)$ acts as a *main instance* while others $tms_{id}(s)$ act as *normal instances* where $s = \{1, ..., \mathcal{N}_{tms}\}$. $tms_{id}(0)$ is responsible for the optimal number of nodes $\mathcal{N}_{tms}$ *estimation*, feedbacks *reallocation*, trust result *caching* (consumer side), availability of each node *prediction*, and the trust management service instance *replication*. $tms_{id}(s)$ are responsible for trust assessment and feedback storage, the trust result *caching* (cloud service side), and frequency table *update*. Figure 5.4 shows the brief process on how the trust management service instances are managed.

Unlike previous work such as in [35] where all of the invocation history records for a certain client is mapped to a particular trust management service instance (e.g., all feedback given to a certain cloud service in our case), in our approach each trust

**Table 5.1** Notation and meanings in Chap. 5

| Notation | Meaning | Notation | Meaning |
|---|---|---|---|
| $\mathcal{O}_p(s_{tms})$ | The operational power for a particular trust management service node | $\mathcal{V}(s_{tms})$ | The number of feedbacks handled by a particular trust management service node |
| $\mathcal{V}(all_{tms})$ | The total number of feedbacks handled by all trust management service nodes | $\mathcal{V}(mean_{tms})$ | The mean of feedbacks handled by all trust management service nodes |
| $e_w(s_{tms})$ | The workload threshold for trust management service nodes | $\mathcal{N}_{tms}$ | The total number of trust management service nodes |
| $1 - F(x)$ | The probability of no failure in $(0, t]$ | $m(x)dx$ | The probability that no failure occurs in any one of the renewal points in interval $(x, x + dx]$ |
| $1 - F(t - x)$ | The probability that no further failure occurs in $(x, t]$ | $f(t)$ | The Laplace transforms of the failure-free function |
| $g(t)$ | The Laplace transforms of the renewal density function | $z(t + 1)$ | The state function |
| $y(t + 1)$ | The measurement function | $\mathcal{D}_w$ | The weight distribution |
| $\mathcal{P}$ | The particle set | $\mathcal{A}(s_{tms}, t)$ | The predicted availability of the trust management service instance |
| $e_a(s_{tms})$ | The availability threshold | $r(s_{tms})$ | The total number of replicas for a particular trust management service instance |
| $e_{Cache}(c)$ | The consumer based caching threshold | $e_{Cache}(s)$ | The cloud service based caching threshold |
| $|\mathcal{V}c(c, s)|_{Cache}$ | The number of new trust feedbacks (i.e., since the last caching update) given by a particular consumer | $|\mathcal{V}(s)|_{Cache}$ | The number of new trust feedbacks (i.e., since the last caching update) given to a particular cloud service |

management service instance (i.e., $tms_{id}(s)$) is responsible for feedbacks given to a set of cloud services where each trust management service instance updates the frequency table. The frequency table shows which trust management service instance is responsible for which cloud service and how many feedbacks it is handling. Example 1 illustrates how feedbacks can be reallocated from one trust management service instance to another. In this example, there are three trust management service instances and the workload threshold $e_w(s_{tms})$ is set to 50 %. The trust management service instance $tms_{id}(1)$ triggers the threshold, therefore based on the steps in the Instances Management Algorithm (see Fig. 5.4), the trust feedbacks for the cloud service (2) are reallocated to $tms_{id}(2)$ (i.e., that has the lowest feedbacks).

| Algorithm: Instances Management Algorithm |
| --- |

1. **Initialization:** $tms_{id}(0)$ computes $\mathcal{O}_p(s_{tms})$ for all trust management service nodes if any

2. **Generation:** $tms_{id}(0)$ estimates $\mathcal{N}_{tms}$ and generates additional trust management service nodes if required

3. **Prediction:** $tms_{id}(0)$ predicts new availability of all trust management service nodes $\mathcal{A}(s_{tms}{}^c t)$ using the Algorithm in Figure 5.1

4. **Replication:** $tms_{id}(0)$ determines $r(s_{tms})$, and generate replicas for each trust management service node

5. **Caching:** $tms_{id}(0)$ starts caching trust results (consumer side) and $tms_{id}(s)$ start caching trust results (cloud service side) using the Algorithm in Figure 5.3

6. **Update:** All $tms_{id}(s)$ update the frequency table

7. **Check Workload 1:** $tms_{id}(0)$ checks whether $e_w(s_{tms})$ is triggered by any $tms_{id}(s)$ before reallocation

**if** $\mathcal{O}_p(s_{tms}) \geq e_w(s_{tms})$ and $\mathcal{V}(s_{tms}) \geq \mathcal{V}(mean_{tms})$ **then**
        go to next step
**else**
        go to step 3
**end if**

8. **Reallocation:**

- $tms_{id}(0)$ asks $tms_{id}(s)$ which triggered $e_w(s_{tms})$ to reallocate all trust feedbacks of the cloud service that has the lowest $|\mathcal{V}(s)|$ to another $tms_{id}(s)$ that has the lowest $\mathcal{V}(s_{tms})$
- perform step 6

9. **Check Workload 2:** $tms_{id}(0)$ computes $\mathcal{O}_p(s_{tms})$ for all trust management service nodes and checks whether $e_w(s_{tms})$ is triggered for any $tms_{id}(s)$ after reallocation

**if** $\mathcal{O}_p(s_{tms}) \geq e_w(s_{tms})$ and $\mathcal{V}(s_{tms}) \geq \mathcal{V}(mean_{tms})$ **then**
        go to step 2
**else**
        go to step 3
**end if**

**Fig. 5.4** Instances management algorithm

**Example 1:**

Reallocation $\left(e_w(s_{tms}) = 50\,\%\right)$

Frequency Table Before Reallocation (Step 1)

$\left(tms_{id}(1), |\mathcal{V}(1)|: 200, |\mathcal{V}(2)|: 150, |\mathcal{V}(3)|: 195\right)$

$\left(tms_{id}(2), |\mathcal{V}(4)|: 30, |\mathcal{V}(5)|: 20, |\mathcal{V}(6)|: 45\right)$

$\left(tms_{id}(3), |\mathcal{V}(7)|: 90, |\mathcal{V}(8)|: 35, |\mathcal{V}(9)|: 95\right)$

Check Workload (Step 2)

$\left(tms_{id}(1), \mathcal{O}_p(1_{tms}): 0.617\right)$

$\left(tms_{id}(2), \mathcal{O}_p(2_{tms}): 0.278\right)$

$\left(tms_{id}(3), \mathcal{O}_p(3_{tms}): 0.205\right)$

Frequency Table After Reallocation (Step 3)

$(tms_{id}(1), |\mathcal{V}(1)|: 200, |\mathcal{V}(3)|: 195)$

$(tms_{id}(2), |\mathcal{V}(2)|: 150, |\mathcal{V}(4)|: 30, |\mathcal{V}(5)|: 20, |\mathcal{V}(6)|: 45)$

$(tms_{id}(3), |\mathcal{V}(7)|: 90, |\mathcal{V}(8)|: 35, |\mathcal{V}(9)|: 95)$

## 5.5   Related Work

Several research works propose availability techniques such as load balancing and caching for trust management frameworks. For instance, Conner et al. [35] proposed a load balancing technique where all of the invocation history records for a certain client is mapped to a particular trust management service instance. They also propose a novel scheme to cache trust values based on recent client activity. The proposed approach is evaluated in both LAN and WAN environments with a realistic application. Xiong and Liu [153] proposed several algorithms for dynamic and approximate computation for caching trust results. They also propose several parameters to measure the credibility of the trust participants feedbacks using trust results of peers. Unlike previous work, in our approach each trust management service instance is responsible for feedbacks given to a set of cloud services where each trust management service instance updates the frequency table (see Sect. 5.4). In addition, in our approach we differentiate the trust management instances responsibilities for efficiently caching the trust results and credibility weights where the main trust management instance caches trust results and credibility weights from the consumer side and the other normal instances caches trust results and credibility weights from the cloud service side using the *Trust Results & Credibility Weights Caching Algorithm* (see Fig. 5.3).

Ensuring the availability of Web services has been an active research area with some good results. Some researchers proposed replication techniques in order to achieve high availability for Web services. For instance, Serrano et al. [129] propose a novel approach for autonomic replication focusing on performance and consistency of Web services that places data copies only on servers close to clients that actually need them. Salas et al. [126] propose WS-Replication, a replication framework for WAN replication of Web services. They propose a WS-Multicast for reliable multicast in a Web services environment. Sheng et al. [130] propose a novel model for on-demand replication decision to decide how many replicas should be created in a dynamic Web services environment. Yao et al. [155] propose a novel approach for predicting the availability of Web services based on a particle filtering technique. They use the concept of service communities to dynamically maintain a subset of Web services with higher availability for compositions purposes. Our work is complementary to these works, particle filtering techniques is used to precisely predict the availability of each node and based on that prediction we can efficiently determine the required number of replicas for each node which will allow any trust management service node to recover any lost data during the down time from its replica. In addition, in our approach we also use load balancing techniques to share the workload, thereby always maintaining a desired availability level where the number of trust management service nodes is determined through an *operational power* metric that we propose.

## 5.6  Summary

In this chapter, we have presented an availability model for scalable and distributed service nodes management, since high availability is an important requirement to the trust management service. We propose to spread several distributed trust management service nodes to manage feedbacks given by consumers in a decentralized way. Load balancing techniques are exploited to share the workload, thereby always maintaining a desired availability level. The number of trust management service nodes is determined through an *operational power* metric that we introduce. In addition, replication techniques are exploited to minimize the possibility of a node hosting a trust management service instance crashing which will allow it to recover any data lost during the down time from its replica. The number of replicas for each node is determined through a *replication determination* metric that we introduce. This metric exploits particle filtering techniques to precisely predict the availability of each node. We further describe the availability model proposed algorithms including *Particle Filtering based Algorithm*, *Trust Results and Credibility Weights Caching Algorithm* and *Instances Management Algorithm*.

We have implemented the proposed availability model and also we conduct extensive experimental and performance studies of the proposed techniques using a collection of real-world trust feedbacks on cloud services. We will report the details of the implementation and experimental evaluation in Chap. 7.

# Chapter 6
# Cloud Service Crawler Engine

In the past few years, cloud computing is gaining a considerable momentum as a new computing paradigm for shifting the service delivery. With cloud computing, users enjoy the option to deploy their services over a network of powerful resource pool with practically no capital investment and modest operating cost [10, 27, 111, 148]. Despite a considerable amount of research works on addressing various challenges in cloud computing such as *data processing and migration* [17, 68, 97, 144], *knowledge management* [57], *accessibility* [151], and *security and privacy* [115, 120], cloud services discovery still largely remains an untouched area [148].

Indeed, with cloud computing, service discovery challenges need to be renewed due to a number of reasons. Firstly, cloud services are offered at different levels, not only providing data or business logic, but also infrastructure capabilities. Currently, there are at least three different service levels which are known as Software as a Service (SaaS), Platform as a Service (PaaS) and Infrastructure as a Service (IaaS). Secondly, the lack of standards for describing and publishing cloud services. Unlike Web services which use standard languages such as the Web Services Description Language (WSDL) to expose their interfaces and the Universal Description, Discovery and Integration (UDDI) to publish their services to services' registries for discovery, the majority of publicly available cloud services are not based on description standards [142, 148] which make the cloud service discovery a challenging problem. For example, some publicly available cloud services do not mention "cloud" at all (such as `Dropbox` [51]). On the other hand, some businesses that have nothing to do with cloud computing (e.g., `cloud9carwash` [34]) may use cloud in their names or service descriptions. Several research questions centered around cloud services discovery are as the following:

Q1:  How to identify whether a service on the Web is a cloud service?
Q2:  How many cloud services are currently available on the Web and who are providing these services? (i.e., are cloud services only provided by major vendors such as Microsoft, IBM, Amazon, Google, etc.)?
Q3:  What kind of cloud service providers are there on the Web?
Q4:  From which part of the world the cloud services are provisioned?
Q5:  To what extent do the established Service-Oriented Computing (SOC) standards contribute to cloud computing?

© Springer International Publishing Switzerland 2014

T. H. Noor et al., *Trust Management in Cloud Services,*
DOI 10.1007/978-3-319-12250-2_6

Q6:    To what extent do consumers trust cloud services?

Q7:    Is there any publicly available cloud service dataset that researchers can use in their cloud computing research?

Based on our observations, we believe that there is a need to identify, collect, and analyze cloud services currently available on the Web. This will help us to understand the current status of cloud services and gain valuable insights on future technical trends in the area.

In this chapter, we describe our proposed *Cloud Service Crawler Engine* (CSCE) [108, 109, 110] for automatic cloud service discovery. To allow cloud service consumers to search for the cloud service that they want to assess and display its trust result, CSCE crawls search engines to collect cloud service information available on the Web, as well as review websites where feedback on cloud services are provided. The collected data will help us validate the proposed techniques (i.e., the techniques in Chaps. 4 and 5) using a collection of real-world trust feedbacks on cloud services. Our crawler engine also has the capabilities to collect, validate, and categorize cloud services. By continuously crawling resources on the Web, it is possible to maintain an up-to-date cloud services repository for an effective and efficient cloud services discovery. To allow the crawler engine to collect, validate, and categorize cloud services, we develop the *Cloud Services Ontology* that facilitates the crawler engine with meta information and describes data semantics of cloud services, which is critical in the sense that cloud services may not necessarily use identifying words (e.g., cloud, infrastructure, platform and software) in their names and descriptions. When developing the cloud services ontology, we consider the cloud computing standard developed by NIST [96].

This chapter is organized as follows. In Sect. 6.1, an overview of the proposed cloud service crawler engine is given. In Sects. 6.2 and 6.3, the cloud services ontology is introduced and the dataset collection is described, respectively. In Sect. 6.4, some main challenges for crawling cloud services are discussed. Finally, some related work are discussed in Sects. 6.5 and 6.6 concludes this chapter.

## 6.1   Design Overview

Figure 6.1 depicts the main components of the cloud service crawler engine, which consists of six different layers, namely the *Cloud Service Providers*, the *Cloud Services Ontology*, the *Cloud Services Seeds Collection*, the *Cloud Services Filtration*, the *Cloud Services Data Extraction*, and the *Cloud Services Storage*.

*Cloud Service Providers Layer.*   This layer (top right part of Fig. 6.1) consists of different cloud service providers who publicly provision and advertise their cloud services on the Web (e.g., IaaS, PaaS, and SaaS). These cloud services are accessible through web-portals and indexed on search engines such as Google, Yahoo, and Baidu. It is interesting to note that there are some websites such as Cloud Hosting Reviews [122] and Cloud Storage Service Reviews [1] that enable

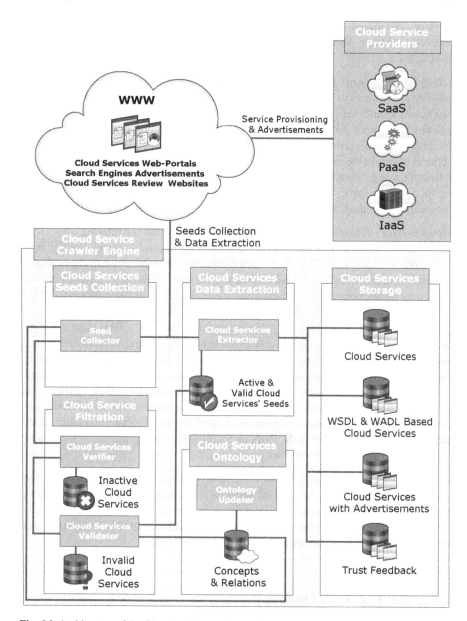

**Fig. 6.1** Architecture of the Cloud service crawler engine

users to provide feedback on cloud services. The potential set of cloud service providers indexed by the various search engines form the initial input to the crawler.

*Cloud Services Ontology Layer.* This layer is responsible for maintaining the *cloud service ontology*. The cloud service ontology contains a set of concepts and relationships to allow the crawler to automatically discover, validate, and categorize cloud services. The maintenance of the ontology is accomplished via a module called the *Ontology Updater*. More information on the cloud services ontology can be found in Sect. 6.2.

*Cloud Services Seeds Collection Layer.*   This layer is responsible for collecting possible cloud services' seeds (i.e., the cloud services' URLs). We develop the *Seed Collector* module that considers several possible resources in search engines such as indexed Web pages, WSDL and Web Application Description Language (WADL)[1] documents, and advertisements. For the data collection, the Seed Collector uses some of the concepts in the first few levels of the Cloud Services Ontology as keywords to collect data (e.g., cloud services, IaaS, PaaS, SaaS, etc.) where the collected seeds are then sent to the *Cloud Services Filtration* layer for validation (i.e., where the knowledge from the Cloud Services Ontology is used for reasoning).

*Cloud Services Filtration Layer* . This layer is responsible for filtering cloud services' seeds collected from the Seed Collector. The *Cloud Services Verifier* first determines whether a cloud service's seed is an active or inactive one. Inactive seeds are kept in the *Inactive Cloud Services* database for another check (i.e., some inactive seeds may be temporarily unavailable) and the error codes are also captured. Active seeds are passed to the *Cloud Services Validator* for validation by using the concepts from the Cloud Services Ontology. For example, if the seed's Web page contains concepts that are related to cloud services such as IaaS, storage, infrastructure, etc., then the seed is considered as a valid one. However, if the seed's Web page contains other concepts such as news, article, paper, weather, etc., then the seed is considered invalid (more details about the concepts can be found in Sect. 6.2). This means that the collected seed could be a news website that publishes articles about cloud services. Invalid seeds are kept in the *Invalid Cloud Service* database and valid seeds are categorized (i.e., either IaaS, PaaS or SaaS) before being passed to the *Cloud Services Data Extraction* for further processing.

*Cloud Services Data Extraction Layer* . This layer is responsible for extracting the information for active and valid cloud services. The cloud services data is stored in the corresponded databases in the *Cloud Services Storage* layer for further analysis. The overall algorithm used by the Cloud Service Crawler Engine (CSCE) for cloud service crawling is summarized in Fig. 6.2.

## 6.2   Cloud Services Ontology

The Cloud Services Ontology (CSO) provides the crawler engine with meta-information and describes common data semantics of cloud services, which is critical in the sense that cloud services may not necessarily use identity words (e.g., cloud,

---

[1] WADL is the REST equivalent of WSDL that can be used to describe RESTful Web services. Unified Service Description Language (USDL) is excluded due to the insufficient results during our initial attempts for cloud service discovery.

---

**Algorithm**: Cloud Service Discovery Algorithm

Step 1. **Ontology:**
The *Ontology Updater* updates the concepts and relations in the *Concepts & Relations* database.

Step 2. **Discovery:**
The *Seed Collector* (SC) gets the (is-a) relations from the *Concepts & Relations* database
SC collects possible seeds for cloud services
SC passes the collected seeds, $\mathcal{S}_c$ to the *Cloud Services Verifier*.

Step 3. **Verification:**
/*The *Cloud Services Verifier* determines whether a cloud service seed is active or inactive*/
**foreach** collected cloud service seed $s \in \mathcal{S}_c$ **do**
    **if** $s$ is inactive **then**
        - capture error code
        - store $s$ in the Inactive Cloud Services database
    **else**
        - pass active seed $s_a$ to the *Cloud Services Validator*
    **end if**
**end foreach**

Step 4. **Validation:**
The Cloud Services Validator gets the (is-not-a/is-a) relations from the *Concepts & Relations* database.
/*The Cloud Services Validator determines whether a cloud service seed is valid or invalid using is-not-a concepts*/
**foreach** active cloud service seed $s_a$ **do**
    **if** cloud service seed $s_a$ is invalid **then**
        - store $s_a$ in the Invalid Cloud Services database
    **else**
        - categorize valid seed $s_{av}$ using is-a concepts
        - pass $s_{av}$ to the Active & Valid Cloud Services Seeds database

    **end if**
**end foreach**

Step 5. **Data Extraction & Storage:**
/*The Cloud Services Extractor extracts data from the valid seed $s_{av}$ and store the data in the corresponding database*/
**foreach** $s_{av}$ **do**
    Store data of $s_{av}$ in the Cloud Services database.
    **if** $s_{av}$ is WSDL or WADL **then**
        - store $s_{av}$'s data in the WSDL & WADL Cloud Services database.
    **else if** $s_{av}$ is advertisement based **then**
        - store $s_{av}$'s data in the Cloud Services with Advertisements database.
    **else if** $s_{av}$ is QoS based **then**
        - store $s_{av}$'s data in the QoS Based Cloud Services database.
    **end if**
**end foreach**

Go to Step 1

---

**Fig. 6.2** Cloud service discovery algorithm

infrastructure, platform and software) in their names and descriptions. When developing CSO, we consider the common concepts that appear in the cloud computing standard developed by the National Institute of Standards and Technology (NIST) [96].

Our CSO contains a set of concepts and relationships between concepts to allow the cloud service crawler engine to automatically discover, validate and categorize cloud services on the Web. CSO is developed based on the Protégé Ontology Editor and Knowledge Acquisition System [117], which is used for constructing the ontology and reasoning the concepts. These concepts enable the cloud service crawler engine to collect possible cloud services' seeds and then filter out invalid seeds (see Fig. 6.2). CSO defines two different relations, namely is-a and is-not-a. For presentation purposes, Fig. 6.3 only shows a small part of the ontology. The Seed Collector uses the concepts in the first few levels of the Cloud Services Ontology as keywords to collect data (e.g., cloud services, IaaS, PaaS, SaaS, etc.) that are associated with is-a relations (see Fig. 6.3a) to collect possible cloud services' seeds from search engines. On the other hand, the Cloud Services Validator uses concepts that are associated with is-not-a relations (see Fig. 6.3) for the cloud services validation. For example, if the seed's Web page contains concepts that are associated with is-not-a relations such as news, article, paper, weather, etc., this means that the collected seed could be a news website that publishes articles about cloud services and should be considered as an invalid seed. Finally, the Cloud Services Validator uses the concepts that are associated with (is-a) relations for categorizing a valid cloud service to either IaaS, PaaS, SaaS, or a combination of these models (i.e., depending on the concepts that appear on the seed's Web page whether it is related to IaaS, PaaS, SaaS or a combination of these cloud services). For example, if the Web page contains several concepts such as OnlineBackup, Datacenter and Webhosting then the Web page is considered an IaaS cloud service.

## 6.3  Datasets Collection

Search engines are the primary source to collect cloud services meta-data since we are not aware of any business registries (such as UDDI registries for Web services) for cloud services. Even for Web services, it is well known that the idea of UDDI business registries is a failure and the discovery of Web services are moving towards search engines [2, 88].

Our cloud services crawler engine explores the Web for cloud services using existing search engines' APIs (e.g., Google, Yahoo, and Baidu). We basically choose the first few levels of the Cloud Services Ontology as keywords to collect data such as Cloud Services, IaaS, PaaS, SaaS, Communication, Storage, Infrastructure, Online Backup, Web Hosting, Virtual Desktop, Virtual Machine, Software, API, etc. The crawler collected possible cloud services' seeds by continuously parsing search results from the indices returned by search engines. The cloud service crawler engine managed to parse 619,474 possible links and discovered 35,601 possible seeds for cloud Services. It should be noted that the discovered cloud services' Web pages are full of noisy data (e.g., wiki, news, articles that are related to cloud services) which need to be filtered. After the filtration process, the cloud service crawler engine identified 5883 unique cloud services, which are kept in the *cloud services* database

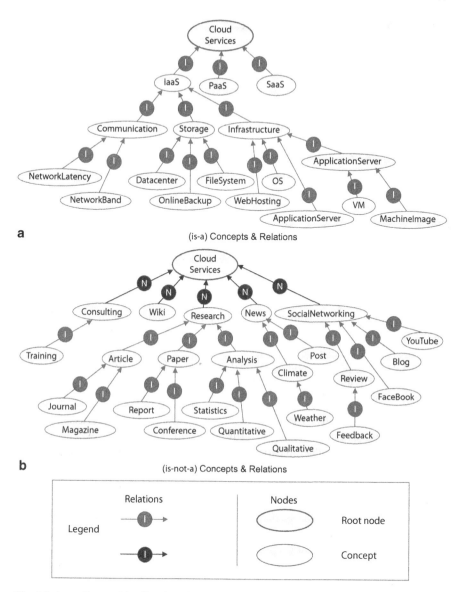

**Fig. 6.3** A small part of the Cloud services ontology

(see Fig. 6.1). From the collected information, we prepared several large datasets of real-world cloud services and will release them to the research community. It is interesting to note that the collected datasets is worth 1.06 GB of cloud services information [108, 110], which will be released to the research community.

*WSDL & WADL Based Cloud Services* . One of important investigations in our mind is to find out how Service-Oriented Computing (SOC) contributed to the cloud

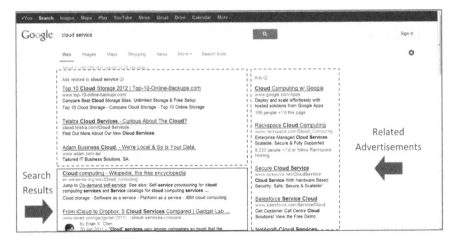

**Fig. 6.4** Advertised Cloud services

computing. For this purpose, we are particularly interested to find out how many
cloud services have been implemented using SOC standards such as WSDL. To
collect this dataset, the cloud service crawler engine is configured to search for
files with extensions such as WSDL and WADL. Our cloud service crawler engine
managed to parse 1552 possible links and discovered 616 possible seeds for cloud
services in WSDL and WADL. After the filtration process, our cloud service crawler
engine identified 106 valid cloud services implemented using WSDL and WADL.

*Cloud Services with Advertisement.* During collection of cloud services, we find
that some cloud service providers advertise their cloud services in search engines,
which usually appear on the top part and/or the right part of the returned index pages
(see Fig. 6.4). Since advertising is an important step for users to discover services,
we are interested to find out what is the portion of cloud services that use this as
a means in publishing and discovering their cloud services, giving the scarcity of
standards on this. To collect this dataset, the cloud service crawler engine collected
possible cloud services' seeds by continuously parsing advertisements that appear
in the top or the right side of the search results from the search engines (i.e., these
advertisements are called Ads or sponsored results), and eventually identified 637
unique cloud services.

*User Trust Feedback.* Finally, because trust is one of the most concerned issues for
adopting cloud computing [10, 111, 148], we are interested to know users' opinions
on real-world cloud services. To collect this dataset, the cloud service crawler engine
investigated some leading review websites such as Cloud Hosting Reviews
[122] and Cloud Storage Reviews [1] and collected cloud service consumers'
feedback on cloud services. The cloud service crawler engine collected 10,076 feedbacks given by 6982 consumers to 113 valid cloud services. The results are kept in
the *trust feedback* database.

## 6.4   Design Challenges

The automatic discovery, verification, validation, collection and categorization of cloud services is not a straightforward task. In order to collect the desired datasets, the design of such a cloud service crawler engine has to overcome several challenges including the following:

*Dynamic Behavior of Cloud Services.*   Cloud services are dynamic in the sense that new cloud services appear on the Web while old cloud services might discontinue around the clock. In addition, cloud services may change over the time. As a result, the crawler engine needs to be able to update or revisit cloud services periodically in order to keep the repository up-to-date. It is important to distinguish between cloud services that must be revisited (e.g., new cloud services and those frequently updated) and those that can be skipped (e.g., discontinued cloud services or those less updated). Due to large amount of possible cloud services on the Web, being able to separate them into different groups will greatly improve the crawling performance.

*Lack of Standardization.*   Unlike Web services that can be discovered by simply collecting WSDL documents or searching the UDDI registries, cloud services lack of standardized description languages which make them harder to discover. This in fact is the most significant challenge in cloud service discovery. The cloud services crawler engine may collect unnecessary and noisy data (e.g., wiki, news, blogs, reviews, and research papers related to cloud). For example, our cloud services crawler engine initially collected 35,601 possible seeds on the Web, only 16.14 % of which (i.e., 5883) are actually cloud services.

*Scalability.*   The number of cloud services available on the Web can be big and is increasingly growing, which can heavily affect the cloud service crawler engine's performance. Therefore, several instances of the cloud service crawler engine need to be running simultaneously from multiple machines in order to optimize the crawling performance. Clearly, there is a need to coordinate these multiple instances to avoid redundant work.

*Crawling Blockage.*   There is a clear trade-off between high performance and re-source consumption. Crawling search engines and some websites may consume resources of other organizations, which can cause the cloud services crawler being blocked from accessing these services. Thus, the cloud service crawler engine needs to enhance its performance without consuming the service providers' resources and minimize the load on network (e.g., using several instances of the crawler from different locations and IP addresses).

## 6.5   Related Work

Service discovery is considered as one of the fundamental approaches in several research areas such as ubiquitous computing, mobile ad-hoc networks, Peer-to-Peer (P2P), and Service-Oriented Computing (SOC) [2, 98, 99, 148]. Although service discovery is a very active research area, particularly in Web services in the past decade, for cloud services, challenges need to be reconsidered and solutions for effective cloud service discovery are very limited [78, 148].

Some researchers propose to use ontology techniques for cloud services discovery. For instance, Kang and Sim [78] propose a Cloud Service Discovery System (CSDS) which exploits ontology techniques to find cloud services that are closer to cloud service consumers' requirements. In particular, the authors propose a cloud ontology where agents are used to perform several reasoning methods such as similarity reasoning, equivalent reasoning and numerical reasoning. Our work is complementary to this work, as their strategies can be modified for use in bigger environments (i.e., the World Wide Web (WWW)). Additionally, our work contributes in the use of a different cloud services ontology where several relations are defined namely is-a and is-not-a that helps in filtering out noisy data and increasing the accuracy of the discovery results (The cloud services ontology is detailed in Sect. 6.2).

Other researchers propose to use Distributed Hash Tables (DHTs) for better discovery and load-balancing of cloud services. For example, Ranjan et al. [119] propose the concept of *cloud peer* that extends DHT overlay to support indexing and matching of multidimensional range queries (i.e., the dimensions can include service type, processor speed, available memory, network bandwidth, etc.) for service discovery. The proposed approach is validated on a public cloud computing platform (Amazon EC2). Their work focuses on a closed environment. In contrast, we focus on discovering cloud services on an open environment (i.e., WWW) to allow users to search cloud services that suite their needs.

Discovering Web services has been an active research area with some good results. Al-Masri and Mahmoud [2] collect WSDL documents by crawling UDDI Business Registries (UBRs) as well as search engines such as Google, Yahoo, and Baidu. The authors analyze the collected data and present some detailed statistical information on Web services such as active versus inactive Web services and object size distribution. Li et al. [84] also collect Web services data through Google API, and present some interesting statistical information related to the operation, size, word distribution and function diversity of Web services. Most recently, Renzel et al. [121] report their findings on the current status of RESTful Web services. The authors use 17 different RESTful service design criteria (e.g., availability of formal description, links in representations, number of resource types, etc.) to analyze the top 20 RESTful services listed on programmableWeb [116]. Unlike previous work where Web services are discovered by simply collecting interface documents (e.g., WSDL files) and searching UDDI business registries, discovering cloud services possesses more challenges such as the lack of standardized description languages for cloud services, which need a full consideration.

## 6.6  Summary

In this chapter, we have presented a cloud service crawler engine for automatic cloud service discovery. Our crawler engine crawls search engines to collect cloud service information available on the Web and has the capabilities to collect, validate, and categorize cloud services. By continuously crawling resources on the Web, it is possible to maintain an up-to-date cloud services repository for an effective and efficient cloud services discovery. Our cloud service crawler parsed 619,474 possible links for cloud services publicly available on the Web and eventually identified and categorized 5883 valid cloud services. To the best of our knowledge, this is the first effort in discovering, collecting, and analyzing cloud services on the WWW scale. The collected datasets, which are to be released, will bring significant benefits to the research community. These collected datasets is worth 1.06 GB [108, 110] of cloud services information.

In order to adequately answer the research questions aforementioned earlier in this chapter, we conduct a set of statistical analysis and present the results in Chap. 7. The statistical analysis includes the distribution on cloud service providers categorization, geographical location and languages, relationship between cloud computing and Service-Oriented Computing (SOC), as well as cloud computing and Quality of Service (QoS). These results offer an overall view on the current status of cloud services.

# Chapter 7
# Implementation and Performance Study

This chapter is devoted to the implementation and performance study of our proposed credibility-based trust management and automatic discovery of cloud services in distributed and highly dynamic environments [106, 108–110]. We implemented these techniques inside the *Cloud Armor* prototype. The Cloud Armor system, aim at providing a comprehensive platform for automatic cloud service discovery, malicious behavior detection, trust-based recommendation of cloud services and high availability support. To validate the feasibility and benefits of our approach, we conduct extensive experimental and performance studies of the proposed techniques using a collection of real-world trust feedbacks on cloud services. First, based on the collected data, we conduct a set of statistical analysis and present the results. These statistical results offer an overall view on the current status of cloud services. Second, we validate and study the performance of our credibility model by studying the effectiveness in distinguishing between feedbacks from experienced and amateur consumers. We study the robustness of the proposed techniques against different malicious behaviors namely: collusion and Sybil attacks under several behaviors and performed several precision and recall measurements. Finally, we validate and study our availability model from various aspects including accuracy and performance.

This chapter is organized as follows. In Sect. 7.1, a brief overview of the Cloud Armor prototype is given and the enabling technologies used in Cloud Armor are described. A demonstration scenario that illustrates the main features of the Cloud Armor system are described in Sect. 7.2. In Sect. 7.3, the statistical analysis and crawling results are reported. The results of a set of experimental evaluations and performance studies of Cloud Armor are reported in Sect. 7.4. Finally, in Sect. 7.5 a summary of the chapter is provided.

## 7.1 Cloud Armor Overview

Cloud Armor provides an environment where consumers can give trust feedback and request trust assessment for a particular cloud service. The platform (Fig. 7.1) exploits a web crawling approach for automatic cloud services discovery, which consists of the following main components:

© Springer International Publishing Switzerland 2014
T. H. Noor et al., *Trust Management in Cloud Services,*
DOI 10.1007/978-3-319-12250-2_7

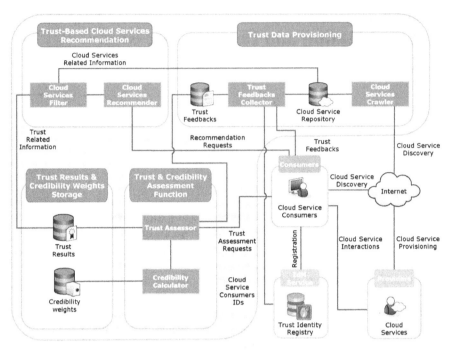

**Fig. 7.1** Cloud Armor's architecture

## 7.1.1  The Trust Data Provisioning Layer

This component is responsible for collecting cloud services and trust information. We developed the *Cloud Services Crawler* module based on the Open Source Web Crawler for Java (crawler4j [39]) and extend it to allow the platform to automatically discover cloud services on the Internet and store cloud services' information (e.g., the cloud service ID, URL and description) in the *Cloud Services Repository* (as mentioned in Chap. 6). We implemented a set of functionalities to simplify the crawling process and make the crawled data more comprehensive (e.g., `addSeeds()` and `selectCrawlingDomain()`). In addition, we developed the *Trust Feedbacks Collector* module to collect trust feedbacks directly from cloud service consumers in the form of history records and stores them in the *Trust Feedbacks Database*. Indeed, the cloud service consumers typically have to establish their identities for the first time they attempt to use the platform through registering their credentials at the *Identity Management Service* (IdM) which stores the credentials in the *Trust Identity Registry* (as mentioned in Chap. 3).

### 7.1.2 The Trust and Credibility Assessment Function Layer

This function is responsible for handling trust assessment requests from users where the trustworthinesses of cloud services are compared and the credibilities of trust feedbacks are calculated. We developed the *Credibility Calculator* to measure the credibility of trust feedbacks based on a set of credibility factors to aggregate the credibility weights. The credibility factors include the cloud service consumer experience (i.e., which is calculated based on the cloud service consumer's capability and the majority consensus factors), feedback density, occasional feedback collusion, multi-identity recognition, occasional Sybil attacks and the change rate of trust factors (more details on how the credibility factors are calculated can be found in Chap. 4). Moreover, we developed the *Trust Assessor* to compare the trustworthiness of cloud services through requesting the aggregated credibility weights from the *Credibility Calculator* to weigh the trust feedbacks and then calculate the mean of all trust feedbacks given to each cloud service. The trust results for each cloud service and the credibility weights for trust feedbacks are stored in the databases (i.e., the *Trust Results and Credibility Weights Storage* in Fig. 7.1) asaforementioned in Chap. 3.

### 7.1.3 The Trust-based Cloud Services Recommendation Layer

This component is responsible for recommending trustworthy cloud services to users. We developed the *Cloud Services Recommender* to recommend trustworthy cloud services that suit the users' needs using the *Cloud Services Filter*. The *Cloud Services Filter* filters cloud services based on the cloud service's category (e.g., Infrastructure as a Service (IaaS), Platform as a Service (PaaS) and Software as a Service (SaaS) based on keywords such as *storage* and *host*) and their corresponding trust results. Consequently, the *Cloud Services Recommender* uses the trust assessment requests from users to recommend trustworthy cloud services that suit requesters' need.

We use state-of-the-art technologies for the implementation of Cloud Armor. Table 7.1 gives a summary of these technologies. In Cloud Armor, the trust management service is deployed as a web application using Netbeans (IDE) [38]. Netbeans provides not only a server-side infrastructure for deploying and managing the trust management service and the identity management service, but also a client-side interface for invoking both services (i.e., where JSP is used to integrate between the Hyper Text Markup Language (HTML) based interface and the Java servlets to be invoked).

In our implementation, we use Apache Tomcat [141] as a Web server and MySQL [112] database application to store the cloud service consumers' identity records (i.e., for the identity management service), the anonymized identity matrix, the Multi-Identity recognition matrix, the cloud service consumers' trust feedbacks and the cloud services' trust results (as mentioned in Chap. 4). We use Java Remote Method Invocation (RMI) [37] to build the decentralized version of Cloud Armor prototype for managing the trust management service instances and

**Table 7.1** Enabling technologies in Cloud Armor

| Product | Version | Usage descriptions |
|---------|---------|---------------------|
| Netbeans | 7.2.1 | Used to develop Cloud Armor web applications and integrate its parts (e.g., Web server with a database) in a single platform |
| Java | JDK 1.7 | Used to implement the Cloud Armor modules as Java servlets (e.g., Identity Management Service's registrar) |
| JSP | NA | Java server page is used to integrate between the HTML and Java servlet that Cloud Armor uses |
| Apache Tomcat | 6 | Web server |
| MySQL | 5.2.34 | Application databases |
| JDBC | 5.1.22 | Database connections |
| Protégé desktop | 3.5 | Ontology editor and knowledge acquisition system used to develop the Cloud Services Ontology |
| crawler4j | 3.3 | Open source Web crawler for Java used to crawl the Internet to allow Cloud Armor to discover cloud services |
| Google chart tools | NA | Used to plot charts that show the trustworthiness behavior of cloud services |
| Highcharts | NA | Used to visualize the cloud services trust feedback information |

reallocating the trust feedbacks based on the proposed algorithms in Chap. 5. In addition, we use Protégé Ontology Editor and Knowledge Acquisition System [117] for developing the *Cloud Services Ontology* to allow Cloud Armor to identify, collect, and analyze cloud services currently available on the Internet. We adopt crawler4j [39] and extend it to develop the *Cloud Services Crawler* module which allows Cloud Armor to automatically discover cloud services on the Internet. We use several visualizing tools including: Google Chart Tools [61] and Highcharts [69] to visualize the trustworthiness behavior of a particular cloud services and to visualize some statistics such as trust feedback information.

As a proof of concept, we provide a demonstration scenario to show the salient features of Cloud Armor including: (i) the innovative use of a web crawling approach for automatic cloud services discovery; (ii) an adaptive and robust credibility model for measuring the credibility of feedbacks; and (iii) a trust-based recommender to recommend trustworthy cloud services that suit the users needs. We also conducted an extensive experimental performance study of Cloud Armor, which will be reported in Sect. 7.4.

## 7.2  Demo Scenario

Cloud Armor provides an environment where cloud service consumers can give trust feedback and request trust assessment for a particular cloud service. In this section, we will focus on demonstrating: (i) how the cloud services are discovered and the trust feedbacks are collected, (ii) how the trust assessment requests are handled and the credibility aggregated weights are configured, and (iii) how the trustworthy cloud services are recommended.

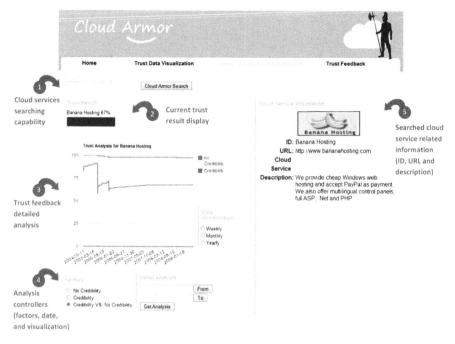

**Fig. 7.2** The Cloud services trust assessment

## 7.2.1 Provisioning Trust Data

The cloud service crawler offers several functionalities that a system administrator can use for cloud service discovery and information collection. The system administrator can add specific keywords for the crawling process, select the domain, and specify the time that the crawler starts the crawling process and the crawling period. The cloud services' information is stored in the *Cloud Services Repository* to be displayed when users search for cloud services (See Fig. 7.2, Area 5). Users can easily search for desirable cloud services and provide feedback to aparticular cloud service.

## 7.2.2 Assessing Trust and Credibility

The Trust Assessor gives cloud service users the ability to search for the cloud service that they want to assess (See Fig. 7.2, Area 1) where the trust result for the searched cloud service is then displayed (See Fig. 7.2, Area 2). In addition, a detailed analysis of the trust feedback for the cloud service is also displayed (See Fig. 7.2, Area 3). Several analysis controllers are provided for users such as credibility factors in calculating the trust result and the ability to visualize the trust results for the cloud service based on different time period (e.g., in day, month, or year) (See Fig. 7.2, Area 4). The credibility calculator allows the administrator to tweak the credibility weights according to the trust assessment preferences.

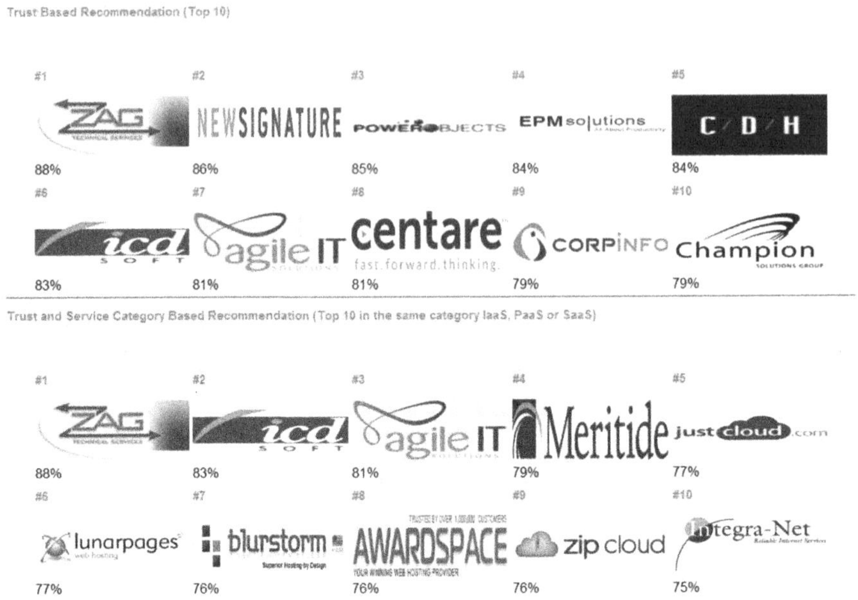

Trust Based Recommendation (Top 10)

Trust and Service Category Based Recommendation (Top 10 in the same category IaaS, PaaS or SaaS)

**Fig. 7.3** Trust-based Cloud services recommendation

### 7.2.3 Recommending Cloud Services Based on Trust Results

The Cloud Service Recommender allows users to receive recommendations of trustworthy cloud services based on the query that they used to search for cloud services (See Fig. 7.2, Area 1). Cloud services are ranked according to their corresponding trust results. The upper part of Fig. 7.3, shows the top ten trustworthy cloud services for all cloud services regardless their category (i.e., IaaS, PaaS or SaaS). The Cloud Services Filter also provides the administrator with several functionalities such as the ability to choose the filtering technique (e.g., to filter the recommended cloud services based on the cloud services' category). The lower part of Fig. 7.3, shows the top ten trustworthy cloud services that are in the same category. The cloud services are categorized using keywords chosen by the administrator (e.g., *Storage, Online Backup,* and *WebHosting* indicate IaaS).

## 7.3 Statistical Analysis and Crawling Results

In this section we present a comprehensive, statistical analysis of the crawling results and the collected data on cloud services, from a number of different aspects. These results also provide some insights to the questions we aforementioned in Chap. 6.

**Table 7.2** Breakdown of Cloud services crawling results

|                | Start page | WSDL/WADL | Ads | Total   |
|----------------|-----------|-----------|-----|---------|
| Links parsed   | 617,285   | 1552      | 637 | 619,474 |
| Possible seeds | 34,348    | 616       | 637 | 35,601  |
| Inactive       | 366       | 57        | 0   | 423     |
| Active         | 34,619    | 559       | 637 | 35,815  |
| Invalid        | 28,736    | 453       | 0   | 29,189  |
| Valid          | 5883[a]   | 106       | 637 | 5883    |

[a]Cloud services identified from WSDL/WADL and Advertisements are also found from the search engines

## 7.3.1   Cloud Services Identification

To optimize the crawling performance, we used three different instances of the cloud service crawler engine (i.e., each instance collects the data using multiple threads) to run simultaneously from three different machines. At an early stage, we configured the crawler to crawl up to five levels deep in a potential cloud service's Website. However, we discontinued doing so because (i) it is time consuming and (ii) there is no significant difference in the crawling results. Therefore, we configured the crawler to crawl the first level of the potential cloud service's Website where the service description was mostly found. Table 7.2 depicts a breakdown of the cloud services collection and verification results.

From the table, we can see that there exists a significant portion of noisy data during the collection. After parsing 619,474 links, the crawler found 29,189 invalid seeds (over 80 %) from 35,601 possible seeds for cloud services. This is largely contributed by the fact that there lacks of standards for describing and publishing cloud services. Therefore, there is an urgent need for standardization on cloud services such as interfacing and discovery. It should be noted that for cloud services extracted from advertisements, there is no noisy data at all. All 637 cloud services collected by our crawler are valid cloud services. Clearly, cloud services from advertisements are likely reliable.

It is also worth mentioning that the total number of inactive cloud services is significantly low (only 423, about 0.1 % of the total possible seeds). This is because search engines regularly check outdated links and exclude them from their indexes. For those inactive cloud services, our crawler also captured the error codes according to the RFC 2616 status code definitions by W3C [118], shown in Table 7.3. From the Table, we can see that the highest percentage (66.95 %) goes to error code 1005 (i.e., the URL does not exist), which means that the majority of inactive cloud services are discontinued.

**Table 7.3** Error codes for inactive Cloud services

| Error code | Description | Percentage |
|---|---|---|
| 101 | The connection was reset | 13.66 |
| 105 | Unable to resolve the server's DNS address | 1.64 |
| 107 | SSL protocol error | 0.27 |
| 118 | The operation timed out | 0.27 |
| 324 | Theserver closed the connection without sending any data | 0.27 |
| 330 | Content decoding failed | 0.27 |
| 400 | Bad request | 0.82 |
| 403 | Access denied | 3.83 |
| 404 | The requested URL/was not found on this server | 10.11 |
| 500 | Server error | 1.37 |
| 503 | The service is unavailable | 0.27 |
| 504 | Page not found | 0.27 |
| 1005 | URL does not exist | 66.95 |
| Total | – | 100 |

## 7.3.2 Locations and Languages

One of our studies about cloud services, and cloud computing in general, is about its *geographical status* (i.e., from which part of the world these cloud services are provisioned). We extracted the country domain from each URL of the collected cloud services. When the country domain is not present in a URL, we exploited *address lookup* tools such as whois [75, 131] to determine the location of the URL, which essentially trace back to the geographical location of the hosting data center and help us to determine the country information for the cloud service. For presentation purposes, we group countries into different regions for a holistic view of cloud computing trends and depict the information on a world map, as shown in Fig. 7.4. For the detailed information about a particular country, we paint it in a specific color, according to the percentage range of the cloud services provisioned by that country.

From Fig. 7.4, we note that North America region is the biggest provider for cloud services, with a percentage of 60.45 %. This is followed by Europe (23.27 %). 8.7 % of the cloud services are provisioned from Asia (about 1 % contributed from the Middle East area) and 5.27 % from Australia. The rest 2.31 % of the cloud services are provisioned from other regions including South America and Africa.

We also conducted some statistics on the languages used for the collected cloud services. We leveraged online tools, What Language is This [56] and an open source system called Language Detection Library for Java [40] for this task. Figure 7.5 shows the statistical information of the languages that are used in the cloud services. From the figure, it is clear that most cloud service providers use English language (garnering 85.33 %). This is consistent with the fact that a large

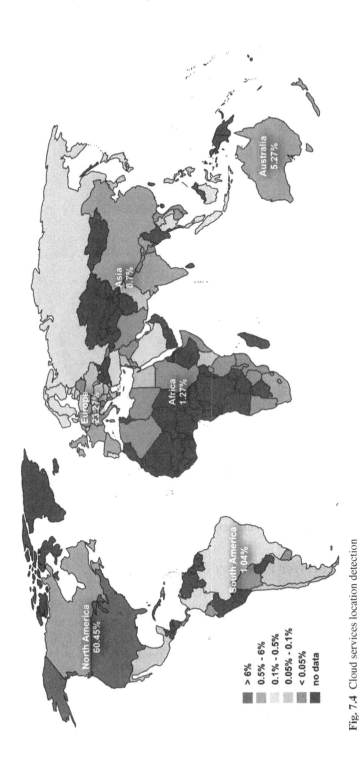

**Fig. 7.4** Cloud services location detection

**Fig. 7.5** Languages used in
Cloud services

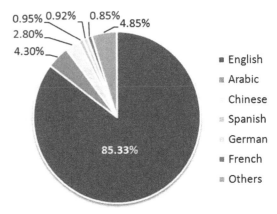

**Fig. 7.6** Cloud service
providers categorization

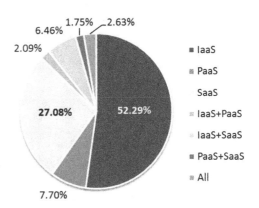

portion of cloud services are provided by countries in North America, Australia, and
Europe (see Fig. 7.4), and most of them are English speaking countries. There is a
substantial adoption of cloud computing, as demonstrated by other languages used
in cloud services such as Chinese, French, German, and Spanish. Noticeably, 4.30 %
of the cloud services are in Arabic language.

### 7.3.3   Cloud Service Providers Categorization

Cloud services are widely categorized into IaaS, PaaS, and SaaS, provisioned by
different cloud service providers. It would be interesting to find out the percentages
of different kinds of cloud service providers. As described in Chap. 6, after our cloud
services crawler finished the validation of cloud service seeds, the crawler categorized
these cloud services into IaaS, PaaS or SaaS by reasoning over the relations between
the concepts in the cloud services ontology (more details on the cloud services
ontology are explained on Sect. 6.2).

Figure 7.6 depicts the categorization results where cloud service providers are
categorized into six different categories, namely, IaaS, PaaS, SaaS, IaaS+PaaS,

**Fig. 7.7** Cloud service
consumers trust feedback

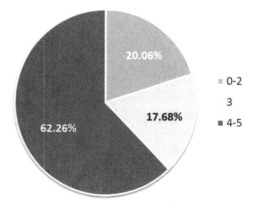

IaaS+SaaS, PaaS+SaaS, and all. It should be noted that when a cloud service provider
is categorized as IaaS+PaaS, it means that this provider offers two types of cloud
services: both IaaS and PaaS services. From the figure, we can see that there is a
fair degree of variety in cloud service providers. In particular, more than half of the
cloud service providers (52.29 %) focus on providing IaaS services, nearly one third
(27.08 %) focus on providing SaaS services and 7.70 % focus on providing PaaS services. The rest 12.93 % offer more than one cloud service models. It should be noted
that those major players such as Microsoft, Amazon, and Googlebelong to this part.

## 7.3.4   Cloud Services and Quality of Service (QoS)

The Quality of Service (QoS) attributes are critical in cloud service discovery. With
QoS information, collected cloud services could be ranked according to consumers'
requirements and the best cloud services are always selected for users or workflow
applications. Our cloud services crawler engine collected cloud services' QoS data
by visiting some review websites that document cloud service consumers' feedback.
Among QoS attributes, we are particularly interested in trust since it is widely
considered as one of the key challenges in the adoption of cloudcomputing [10, 74,
102, 111].

We analyzed 10,076 feedbacks collected from 6982 users on 113 real cloud services. Figure 7.7 depicts the result. Cloud service consumers gave trust feedback
on cloud services in numerical form with a range between 0 and 5, where 0 and
5 mean the most negative and the most positive respectively. From the Figure we
can make a very interesting observation that the majority of the cloud service consumers (62.26 %) are positive (scoring 4–5) in trusting the cloud services they used.
Only 20.06 % of the cloud service consumers' are negative (scoring between 0–2)
in trusting cloud services and the rest (17.68 %) of the consumers' feedbacks are
neutral.

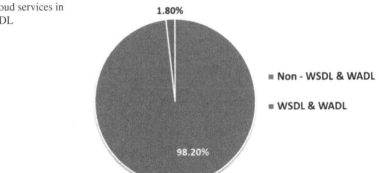

**Fig. 7.8** Cloud services in WSDL/WADL

## 7.3.5   Cloud Computing and Service-Oriented Computing (SOC)

Service-Oriented Computing (SOC) and Web services are believed to be one of the most important enabling technologies for cloud computing [47, 103, 148]. Thus, it is quite interesting to investigate the adoption of SOC in cloud computing. In this work, we conducted some preliminary studies based on the information we collected. We first investigated how much the description languages from SOC such as Web Services Description Language (WSDL) or Web Application Description Language (WADL) have been used for publishing cloud services. To do so, we compared the number of cloud services that have WSDL (i.e., for Simple Object Access Protocol (SOAP) based Web services) or WADL (i.e., for Representational State Transfer (RESTful) Web services) documents. Figure 7.8 depicts the result. It is a big surprise to find out that only a very small portion of cloud services (merely 1.80 %) were implemented using Web service interface languages. However, we would like to point out that cloud services that actually used SOC might not be detected by our crawler because not all WSDL documents are publicly accessible on the Internet [2]. In addition, the majority of RESTful Web services provides no formal descriptions and relies on informal documentation [121]. Nevertheless, the very low percentage still indicates the poor adoption of SOC in cloud computing.

We also investigated how cloud services advertise themselves so that potential customers can find them. In addition to being indexed by search engines, we find that some cloud service providers advertise their services on search engines. These advertisements are usually located on the top and/or the right side of the returned search pages (as mentioned in Chap. 6). Accordingly, our cloud services crawler engine collected those advertised cloud services. Figure 7.9 shows that about 10.80 % of the collected cloud services use paid advertisements as a means for customers to discover them. Since advertised cloud services rely only on a short description text to introduce themselves, user queries that normally require more information (e.g., functions and QoS information of cloud services) cannot be answered via these advertisements.

**Fig. 7.9** Cloud services
advertised on search engines

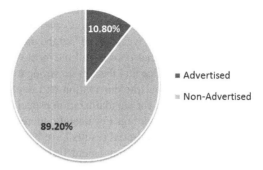

**Fig. 7.10** Cloud services' IPs

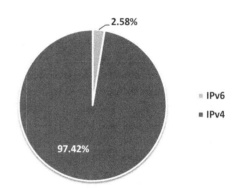

Another interesting and important aspect worth investigating is the cloud services communication (i.e., what type of IPs do cloud services use). An `nslookup` command is used to determine what type of IP cloud services are using (i.e., IPv4 or IPv6). We wrote a simple Java program to enable automatic retrieval of such IP addresses from the collected URLs. As shown in Fig. 7.10, the majority of the cloud services (97.42 %) use IPv4. This does make sense because IPv4 is still the most widely deployed Internet Layer protocol.

### 7.3.6   Discussion

From our analysis we can make a number of interesting observations. First, we can see that although cloud service are provisioned using three models (i.e., IaaS, PaaS, SaaS), 91.79 % of cloud service providers either provision IaaS alone or as part of the provisioned cloud services. Second, we can observe that 79.94 % of cloud service consumers actually do trust cloud services and that cloud be indicated from their high feedbacks on cloud services (i.e., 3-5/5). This is particularly interesting because it is against the statement "trust is one of the most concerned issues for adopting cloud computing", that many researchers agree about [10, 111, 148]. Although the collected data only shows part of the story but still could be considered as an indicator. Third, we can note that the majority of cloud services (97.42 %) uses IPv4 which means that IPv4 is still the most widely deployed Internet Layer protocol. Finally, we notice that there is no strong evidence showing that SOC is playing an active role in the implementation and deployment of cloud services. There is also an urgent need for standardization especially in description languages to fully embrace cloud computing. Fortunately, there are some attempts from the research community and some initial results have been achieved in standardization. For example, the Distributed Management Task Force (DMTF) just released, on 29 August 2012, the Cloud Infrastructure Management Interface (CIMI) specification, which standardizes interactions between cloud environments to achieve interoperable cloud infrastructure management [48].

With the growing adoption of cloud computing, efficiently finding relevant cloud services is becoming an important research issue. The most intriguing finding is the fact that SOC is not playing a significant role in enabling cloud computing as a technology contrary to what is documented in the current literature. More investigation should be conducted in order to understand why this is the case and how to enable SOC to contribute towards cloud computing so as to capitalize on previous efforts in the research and development in SOC communities. In addition, the lack of standardization in the current cloud products and services makes cloud services discovery a more difficult task and a barrier for scalable and unified accessto cloud services.

## 7.4  Experimental Evaluations and Performance Studies

We conducted experiments using the implemented Cloud Armor prototype system. This section presents two sets of experimental results. The first set of experiments were developed to validate and study the performance of the credibility model (see Chap. 4) including: (i) Consumer Experience Determination; (ii) Robustness Against Collusion Attacks; and (iii) Robustness Against Sybil Attacks. The second set of experiments were developed to validate and study the performance of the availability model (see Chap. 5) including: (i) Availability Prediction Accuracy; (ii) Trust Results Caching Accuracy; and (iii) Reallocation Performance.

### 7.4.1  Credibility Model Experiments

We validated our credibility model using real-world trust feedbacks on cloud services. We crawled review websites such as Cloud Hosting Reviews [122] and Cloud Storage Service Reviews [1] where consumers usually give their feedback on cloud services that they used. The collected data represents consumers feedback based on several Quality of Service (QoS) parameters including availability, security, response time, etc. We managed to collect 10,076 feedbacks given by 6982 consumers to 113 real-world cloud services. The collected dataset will be released to the research community in the Cloud Armor project website[1].

For consumer experience determination experiments, we select a group of cloud services which consists of feedbacks given by 100 consumers. This group is used to validate the consumer experience determination in the credibility model. We evaluate our credibility model by comparing trust results when considering the *Consumer Experience* and without considering the *Consumer Experience* factors (i.e., we turn the $Exp(c)$ to 1 for all cloud service consumers). We also compare trust results for each factor in the *Consumer Experience* factors including the *Consumer Capability* and the *Majority Consensus* (more details on how these factors are calculated can be found in Sect. 4.1). For robustness against attacks (i.e., collusion and Sybil Attacks) experiments, the collected data is divided into 6 groups of cloud services, 3 of which are used to validate the credibility model against collusion attacks, and the other 3 groups are used to validate the model against Sybil attacks where each group consists of 100 consumers. Each cloud service group is used to represent a different attacking behavior model, namely: *Waves*, *Uniform* and *Peaks* as shown in Fig. 7.11.

The behavior models represent the total number of malicious feedbacks introduced in a curtain time instance (e.g., $|\mathcal{V}(s)| = 60$ malicious feedbacks when $\mathcal{T}_f = 40$, Fig. 7.11a when experimenting against collusion attacks. The behavior models also represent the total number of identities established by attackers in a period of time (e.g., $|\mathcal{I}(s)| = 78$ malicious identities when $\mathcal{T}_i = 20$, Fig. 7.11c) where one malicious feedback is introduced per identity when experimenting against Sybil attacks. In collusion attacks, we simulated malicious feedback to increase trust results of cloud services (i.e., self-promoting attack) while in Sybil attacks we simulated malicious feedback to decrease trust results (i.e., slandering attack). To evaluate the robustness of our credibility model with respect to malicious behaviors (i.e., collusion and Sybil attacks), we use two experimental settings: (I) measuring the robustness of the credibility model with a conventional model $Con(s, t_0, t)$ (i.e., turning $C_r(c, s, t_0, t)$ to 1 for all trust feedbacks), and (II) measuring the performance of our model using two measures namely *precision* (i.e., to know how well the trust management service did in detecting attacks) and *recall* (i.e., to know how many detected attacks are actual attacks). In our experiments, the trust management service starts rewarding cloud services that have been affected by malicious behaviors when the attacks percentage reaches 25 % (i.e., $e_t(s) = 25\%$), so the rewarding process will occur only when there is a significant damage in the trust result. We have conducted 12 experiments where 6 of which are conducted to evaluate the robustness of our credibility model against collusion attacks and the other 6 for Sybil attacks. Each experiment is denoted by a letter (e.g., $A, B, C$, etc.) as shown in Table 7.4.

---

[1] http://cs.adelaide.edu.au/~cloudarmor.

**Fig. 7.11** Attacking behavior
models

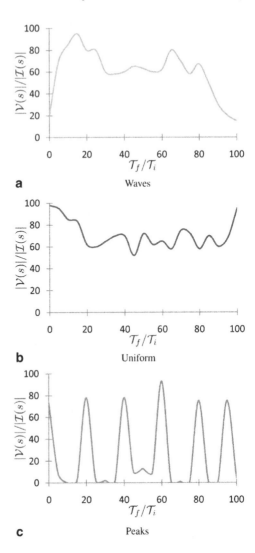

### 7.4.1.1  Consumer Experience Determination

Figure 7.12 depicts the comparison of the trust results when considering the consumer experience and without considering the consumer experience factors. From the figure, it can be seen that the trust results are oscillating more significantly when calculating the trust without considering our approach than when calculating the trust with the consumer experience factors. Even if the trust management service receives inaccurate trust feedbacks from amateur cloud service consumers, it is difficult to manipulate the trust results by using our *Consumer Experience* factors. In other words, our credibility model managed to distinguish between feedbacks from amateur and experience cloud service consumers.

**Table 7.4** Behavior experimental design

| Malicious behaviors | Experimental setting | Waves | Uniform | Peaks |
|---|---|---|---|---|
| Collusion | I | A | B | C |
| Attacks | II | A' | B' | C' |
| Sybil | I | D | E | F |
| Attacks | II | D' | E' | F' |

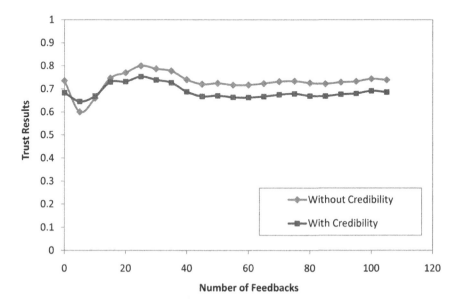

**Fig. 7.12** With consumer experience factors vs. without consumer experience factors

Figure 7.13 shows the comparison of the trust results when only considering the consumer capability factor and when only considering the majority consensus. We can note that the trust results obtained by only considering the consumer capability factor are higher than the trust results by only considering the majority consensus factor. This is true, because we use the consumer capability factor as a reward factor and the majority consensus factor as a penalty factor. This reflects how adaptive our credibility model is where the consumer experience factors can easily be tweaked according to the trust management service's needs. For instance, for optimistic situations where only a few cloud service consumers have high values of capability, increasing the consumer capability factor (i.e., $\beta$) will help the trust management service to distinguish between experienced and inexperienced ones. On the other hand, for pessimistic situations where many consumers have high values of capability, the majority consensus factor (i.e., $\mu$) needs to be increased.

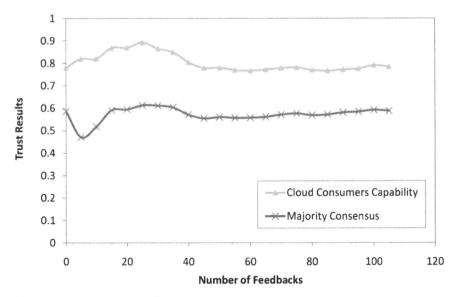

**Fig. 7.13** Consumer capability factor vs. majority consensus factor

### 7.4.1.2   Robustness Against Collusion Attacks

For the collusion attacks experiments, we simulated malicious consumers to increase trust results of cloud services (i.e., self-promoting attack) by giving malicious feedback with the range of [0.8, 1.0]. Figure 7.14 depicts the analysis of 6 experiments which are conducted to evaluate the robustness of our model with respect to collusion attacks. In Fig. 7.14a, b, and c show the trust result for experimental setting $I$, while a′, b′, and c′ depict the result for experimental setting $II$.

We note that the closer to 100 the time instance is, the higher the trust results are when considering to calculate the trust based on the conventional model. This happens because malicious users are giving misleading feedback to increase the trust result for cloud services. On the other hand, the trust results show nearly no change when considering to calculate the trust based on the credibility model (Fig. 7.14a, b and c). This demonstrates that our credibility model is sensitive to collusion attacks and is able to detect such malicious behaviors. In addition, we can make an interesting observation that our credibility model gives the best results in precision when the *Uniform* behavior model is used (i.e., 0.51, see Fig. 7.14b′), while the highest recall score is recorded when the *Waves* behavior model is used (i.e., merely 0.9, see Fig. 7.14a′). Overall there is a fair degree in recall scores when all behavior models are used which indicate that most of the detected attacks are actual attacks. This means that our model can successfully detect collusion attacks (i.e., whether the attack is strategic such as in *Waves* and *Uniform* behavior models or occasional such as in the *Peaks* behavior model) and the trust management service manged to dilute the increased trust results from self-promoting attacks using the proposed credibility factors.

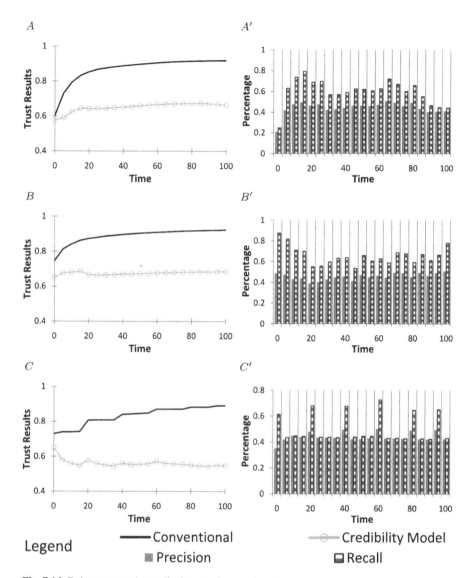

**Fig. 7.14** Robustness against collusion attacks experiments

### 7.4.1.3 Robustness Against Sybil Attacks

For the Sybil attacks experiments, we simulated malicious consumers to decrease trust results of cloud services (i.e., slandering attack) by establishing multiple identities and giving one malicious feedback with the range of [0, 0.2] per identity. Figure 7.15 depicts the analysis of six experiments which are conducted to evaluate the robustness of our model with respect to Sybil attacks. In Fig. 7.15d, e, and f show

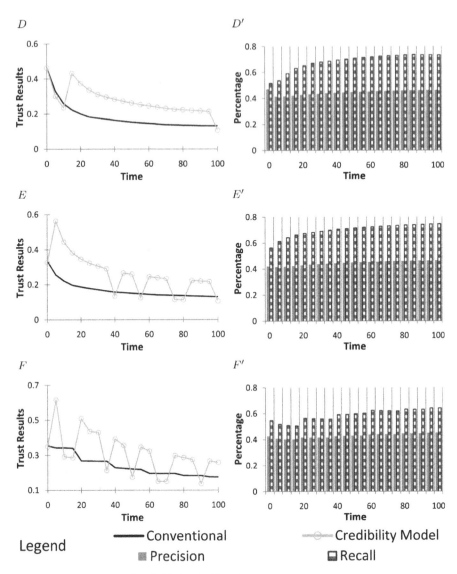

**Fig. 7.15** Robustness Against Sybil Attacks Experiments

the trust result for experimental setting $I$, while d', e', and f' depict the result for experimental setting $II$.

From Fig. 7.15, we can observe that trust results obtained by considering the conventional model decrease when the time instance becomes closer to 100. This is because of malicious users who are giving misleading feedback to decrease the trust result for cloud services. On the other hand, trust results obtained by considering our credibility model are fairly higher than the ones obtained by considering the conventional model (Fig. 7.15d, e and f). This is because the cloud service was rewarded when the attacks occurred. We also can see some sharp drops in trust results obtained by considering our credibility model where the highest number of drops is recorded when the *Peaks* behavior model is used (i.e., we can see 5 drops in Fig. 7.15f which actually matches the drops in the *Peaks* behavior model in Fig. 7.11c. This happens because the trust management service will only reward the affected cloud services if the attacks percentage during the same period of time has reached the attacks percentage threshold (i.e., which is set to 25 % in this case). This means that the trust management service has rewarded the affected cloud service using the change rate of trust results factor. Moreover, from Fig. 7.15d', e' and f', we can see that our credibility model gives the best results in precision when the *Waves* behavior model is used (i.e., 0.47, see Fig. 7.14d'), while the highest recall score is recorded when the *Uniform* behavior model is used (i.e., 0.75, see Fig. 7.14a'). This indicates that our model can successfully detect Sybil attacks (i.e., either strategic attacks such as in *Waves* and *Uniform* behavior models or occasional attacks such as in the *Peaks* behavior model) and the trust management service is able to reward the affected cloud service using the change rate of trust results factor.

## 7.4.2 Availability Model Experiments

We validated our availability model using the same dataset we collected to validate the credibility model. However, for the availability experiments we focused on validating the availability prediction accuracy, trust results caching accuracy, and reallocation performance of the availability model. The experiments are conducted to particularly validate the proposed algorithms including particle filtering based algorithm, trust results & credibility weights caching algorithm and instances management algorithm (more details on the proposed algorithms can be found in Chap. 5).

### 7.4.2.1 Availability Prediction Accuracy

To measure the availability prediction accuracy of the availability model, we simulated 500 nodes hosting trust management service instances and set the failure probability for the nodes as 3.5 %, which complies with the findings in [79]. The reason of this experiment is to study the estimation accuracy of our approach, we simulated the trust management service nodes' availability fluctuation and tracked their fluctuation of availability for 100 time steps (each time step counted as an *epoch*). The actual availability of the trust management service nodes and corresponding estimated availability using our particle filter approach were collected and compared. Figure 7.16 shows the result of one particular trust management service node. From the figure, we can see how fairly close the estimated availability is from the actual availability of the trust management service node. This means that our approach works well in tracing and predicting the availability of the trust management service nodes.

**Fig. 7.16** Availability
prediction accuracy: actual
availability vs. estimated
availability

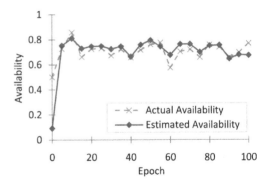

**Fig. 7.17** Trust results
caching accuracy

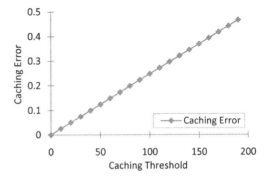

### 7.4.2.2 Trust Results Caching Accuracy

In order to measure the trust results caching accuracy of the availability model, we vary the caching threshold to identify the optimal number of new trust feedbacks that the trust management service receives to recalculate the trust result for a particular cloud service without having a significant error in the trust results (i.e., instead of computing the trust result every time the trust management service receives a trust assessment request from a user). The trust result caching accuracy is measured by estimating the root-mean-square error (RMSE) (denoted caching error) of the estimated trust result and the actual trust result of a particular cloud service. The lower the RMSE value means higher accuracy in the trust result caching. Figure 7.17 shows the trust result caching accuracy of one particular cloud service. From the figure, we can see that the caching error increases almost linearly when the caching threshold increases. This Figure can allow us to choose the optimal caching threshold based on an acceptable caching error rate. For example, if 10 % is an acceptable error margin, then the caching threshold can be set to 50 feedbacks. It is worth mentioning that the caching error was measured on real consumers' feedbacks on real cloud services.

**Fig. 7.18** Reallocation
performance

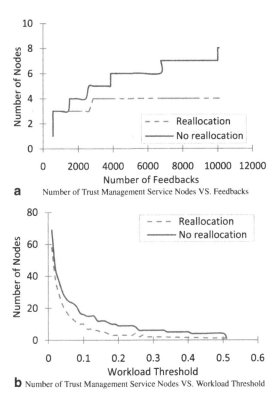

**a** Number of Trust Management Service Nodes VS. Feedbacks

**b** Number of Trust Management Service Nodes VS. Workload Threshold

### 7.4.2.3 Reallocation Performance

To validate the reallocation performance of the availability model, we use two experimental settings: (I) comparing the number of trust management service nodes when using the Reallocation of trust feedbacks and without while increasing the number of feedbacks (i.e., when the workload threshold $e_w(s_{tms}) = 25\%$); (II) comparing the number of trust management service nodes when using the Reallocation of trust feedbacks and without while varying $e_w(s_{tms})$. The lower the number of trust management service nodes the more cost efficient the trust management service is. Figure 7.18a shows the results of experimental settings I. We can observe that the total number of trust management service nodes when using the reallocation of trust feedbacks technique is fairly low and much stable than the total number of trust management service nodes when reallocation is not used (i.e., even when the total number of feedbacks is high). Figure 7.18b shows the results of experimental settings II. From the Figure, we can see that the higher the workload threshold the lower the number of trust management service nodes. However, the number of trust management service nodes when using the reallocation of trust feedbacks technique is lower than the total number of trust management service nodes when reallocation is not considered. This means that our approach works well in minimizing the bandwidth cost by reducing the total number of trust management service nodes as much as possible.

## 7.5   Summary

In this chapter, we have presented the implementation of our proposed techniques in the prototype system *Cloud Armor*. During the implementation, a number of state-of-the-art technologies have been used and tested in our system. To validate the feasibility and benefits of our proposed approaches, we conduct extensive experimental and performance studies of the proposed techniques using a collection of real-world trust feedbacks on cloud services. The experimental results shows that our system (i) is able to effectively distinguish between feedbacks from experienced and amateur consumers; (ii) is more adaptive and robust in trust calculations by effectively detecting collusion and Sybil attacks without breaching consumers' privacy no matter attacks occur in a strategic or occasional behavior; (iii) is more scalable and maintains a desired availability level in highly dynamic environments and (iv) provides an efficient support for identifying, collecting, validating, categorizing and recommending cloud services based on trust.

# Chapter 8
# Conclusions

In the recent years, cloud computing is gaining a considerable momentum as a new computing paradigm for providing flexible and on-demand infrastructures, platforms and software as services. The trust management of services issues attracted many researchers in the past years [26, 35, 66, 89, 135]. However, in cloud computing, with the highly dynamic, distributed and non-transparent nature of cloud services, this research area has gained a considerable significance. Robust trust management approaches will be essential in establishing trust between cloud service consumers and providers and will significantly contribute to the adoption and growth of cloud computing.

In this book, we have proposed a framework for credibility-based trust management and discovery of cloud services. We also provide an implementation of our approach in the *Cloud Armor* (CLOud consUmers' creDibility Assessment & tRust manageMent of clOud seRvices) prototype [109]. In Cloud Armor, the trust is delivered as a service where the trust management service spans several distributed nodes to manage feedbacks in a decentralized way. Cloud Armor exploits crawling techniques for automatic cloud service discovery, credibility techniques for malicious behavior detection, and distributed techniques for high availability support. In particular, we summarize our main research contributions in the following:

- *Zero-Knowledge Credibility Proof Protocol*: Since that preserving the privacy is crucial for the adoption of cloud computing and the development of any services which involves consumers' data (i.e., consumers' identity attributes and interaction histories in our case), we introduced the *Zero-Knowledge Credibility Proof Protocol* (ZKC2P) [106, 107] that not only preserves the consumers' privacy, but also enables the trust management service to prove the credibility of a particular consumer's feedback. We proposed that the Identity Management Service (IdM) can help the trust management service in measuring the credibility of trust feedbacks without breaching consumers' privacy. Anonymization techniques are exploited to protect consumers from privacy breaches in consumers' identities or interactions.
- *Robust and Adaptive Feedback Credibility Assessment*: The credibility of feedbacks plays an important role in the trust management service's performance.

© Springer International Publishing Switzerland 2014
T. H. Noor et al., *Trust Management in Cloud Services*,
DOI 10.1007/978-3-319-12250-2_8

Therefore, we introduce a credibility model for robust and adaptive feedback credibility assessment. We propose several metrics for distinguishing between feedbacks from experienced and amateur consumers including *Consumer Capability* and *Majority Consensus* [103, 104].

We further proposed several metrics for the feedback collusion detection including the *Feedback Density* and *Occasional Feedback Collusion* [102, 105–107]. These metrics distinguish between misleading feedbacks from malicious users and credible ones from normal consumers. It also has the ability to detect strategic and occasional behaviors of collusion attacks (i.e., attackers who intend to manipulate the trust results by giving multiple trust feedbacks to a certain cloud service in a long or short period of time).

In addition, we proposed several metrics for the Sybil attacks detection including the *Multi-Identity Recognition* and *Occasional Sybil Attacks* [105–107]. These metrics allow the trust management service to identify misleading feedbacks from Sybil attacks (i.e., that occur strategically and occasionally). To adjust trust results for cloud services that have been affected by malicious behaviors, we introduced the metric of *Change Rate of Trust* [105, 106] that compensate the affected cloud services by the same percentage of damage.

- *Scalable and Distributed Service Nodes Management*: High availability is an important requirement to the trust management service. Thus, we introduce an availability model for scalable and distributed service nodes management. We propose to spread several distributed trust management service nodes to manage feedbacks given by consumers in a decentralized way. Load balancing techniques are exploited to share the workload, thereby always maintaining a desired availability level. The number of trust management service nodes is determined through an *operational power* metric that we introduce. In addition, replication techniques are exploited to minimize the possibility of a node hosting a trust management service instance crashing which will allow it to recover any data lost during the down time from its replica. The number of replicas for each node is determined through a *replication determination* metric [102, 104] that we introduce. This metric exploits particle filtering techniques to precisely predict the availability of each node.

- *Cloud Service Crawler Engine (CSCE)*: We developed a *Cloud Service Crawler Engine* (CSCE) [108–110] that crawls search engines to collect cloud service information available on the Web. Our crawler engine has the capabilities to collect, validate, and categorize cloud services. By continuously crawling resources on the Web, it is possible to maintain an up-to-date cloud services repository for an effective and efficient cloud services discovery.

  To allow the crawler engine to collect, validate, and categorize cloud services, we developed the *Cloud Services Ontology* that facilitates the crawler engine with meta information and describes data semantics of cloud services, which is critical in the sense that cloud services may not necessarily use identifying words (e.g., cloud, infrastructure, platform and software) in their names and descriptions. When developing the cloud services ontology, we considered the cloud computing standard developed by NIST [96].

- *Datasets Collection*: Based on our observations, we believed that there is a need to identify, collect, and analyze cloud services currently available on the Web. This will help us to understand the current status of cloud services and gain valuable insights on future technical trends in the area. We used the cloud service crawler engine to do this task and the crawler managed to parse 619,474 possible links and discovered 35,601 possible seeds for cloud services. From the collected information, we prepared several large datasets of real-world cloud services and will release them to the research community. These datasets include nearly 6000 cloud services (1.06 GB) [108, 110].
- *Implementation and Performance Study*: We provided an implementation of our proposed framework for credibility-based trust management of cloud services in the *Cloud Armor* prototype [106, 108–110]. In Cloud Armor, the Trust is delivered as a Service (TaaS) where the trust management service spans several distributed nodes to manage feedbacks in a decentralized way. We developed a comprehensive platform for automatic cloud service discovery, malicious behavior detection, trust-based recommendation of cloud services and high availability support.

  To validate the feasibility and benefits of our approach, we conducted extensive experimental and performance studies of the proposed techniques using a collection of real-world trust feedbacks on cloud services. First, based on the collected data, we conducted a set of statistical analysis and presented the results. These statistical results offer an overall view on the current status of cloud services. Second, we validate and study the performance of our credibility model by studying the effectiveness in distinguishing between feedbacks from experienced and amateur consumers, as well as studying the robustness of the proposed techniques against different malicious behaviors namely: collusion and Sybil attacks under several behaviors and performed several precision and recall measurements. Finally, we validated and studied our availability model from various aspects including accuracy and performance.

## 8.1 Future Directions

Although trust management of cloud services issues attracted many researchers, several research issues still need to be addressed. In particular, we identify the following directions for future research in trust management of cloud services.

- *Identification*: Since there is a strong relationship between credibility and identification as emphasized in [43], it is crucial that trust management systems effectively identify cloud service consumers and providers in order to (i) evaluate the credibility of entities (e.g., a cloud service's credibility) and trust feedbacks (more details are explained in Sect. 2.2.1.1) and (ii) protect the integrity of the trust management system's parallel data (i.e., feedback) processing. However, based on the statistical information of the representative research prototypes in Sect. 2.4.2, we note that many of the research prototypes (66 %) do not use any mechanisms to identify credible feedbacks in their trust models. In the cloud environment, credible feedbacks identification is becoming a significant challenge because of the overlapping interactions between the cloud service providers and consumers. The need to determine credible feedbacks will require appropriate strategies such as the one used in *SecureMR* [147] where a novel decentralized replication-based integrity verification scheme for running MapReduce is proposed.

- *Privacy*: Privacy is a fundamental concern in cloud computing. In particular, managing trust in cloud environments requires trust management systems to deal with the cloud service consumers' personal information. Cloud service consumers face several privacy threats such as (i) leaking information pertaining to personal property (e.g., user names, passwords, date of birth, address, etc.) and (ii) tracking consumers' behaviors (e.g., with whom they interacted, which cloud services they used, etc.). According to the statistical information in Sect. 2.4.2, 52 % of the research prototypes do not have any particular mechanism for preserving the privacy of participants. There is therefore a strong need for efficient techniques in preserving privacy of participants but with full consideration of the trust management system availability. One way to preserve privacy is to use cryptographic encryption techniques but there is no efficient way to process encrypted data [115]. Another way is to adopt privacy techniques such as the ones used for *Airavat* [125] where a new approach integrating the mandatory access control and differential privacy is proposed for running MapReduce on Amazon EC2. The differential privacy technique could be used to ensure that the trust result of a cloud service does not violate the privacy of a cloud service consumer who gives the feedback. Fung et al. [60] overview several approaches for preserving privacy in data publishing and we believe that extensive work is needed for developing effective and efficient solutions for privacy protection in the cloud.

- *Personalization*: Cloud services provision several technologies for the same context (e.g., security) and the choice is up to the cloud service consumers (e.g., the use of Virtual Private Network (VPN) or Secure Socket Layer (SSL) for Infrastructure as a Service (IaaS), Platform as a Service (PaaS) and Software as a Service (SaaS) such as in IBM, Password-based protection or Secure Shell (SSH) for IaaS such as in Amazon) regardless if the cloud service consumer is a service provider or a service requester (i.e., these technologies are not suitable for all cloud service consumers). We therefore argue that there is a need for flexible techniques to help cloud service consumers in personalizing the provisioned technologies according to their specific needs. In addition, the number of technologies provisioned by cloud services might be large, which means that a cloud service consumer may face configuration difficulties when using cloud services (e.g., the number of virtual machines, the type of virtual machines, time of tenancy, and access control polices). As a result, there is a strong need for intelligent techniques to make the cloud platform learn the patterns that cloud service consumers usually use. In Sect. 2.4.2, we note that a high proportion of research prototypes (76 %) does not consider the personalization aspect in their trust models and only 24 % of research prototypes use partial personalization in their trust models. Consequently, trust personalization is becoming increasingly important. Trust management systems that support personalization should ensure that participants (i) have the control over their trust feedbacks, (ii) have their own personalized assessment criteria, (iii) have the control over their trust results, and (iv) have the flexibility to change their feedback processes.

- *Integration*: In the cloud environment, trusted parties can give their feedback from different perspectives (e.g., cloud service provider or cloud service consumer) using different techniques (e.g., reputation, policy, etc). Thus, it is important that trust management systems can make use of feedbacks by combining several techniques (e.g., the combination of the reputation technique and the recommendation technique can increase the accuracy of trust results). Combining trust management perspectives can lead to better trust results by matching appropriate service requesters to the trustworthy service providers. Unfortunately, we observe in Sect. 2.4.2 that the majority of the research prototypes (72 %) do not make use of feedbacks integration. As a result, we believe that novel approaches that combine different trust management techniques and make use of feedbacks integration are needed to improve trust results.

- *Security*: Security is a critical issue for cloud computing to be adopted and must be enforced to give businesses the confidence that their data are safely handled. However, it is not unusual that a cloud service experiences malicious behaviors from its users. Due to the dynamic interactions and the distributed nature of cloud environments, it is difficult to know from whom the attack (e.g., whitewashing, self-promoting, and slandering attacks) is expected. Therefore, it is crucial that the trust management systems reliably identify malicious behaviors and mitigate such attacks. Similarly, from Sect. 2.4.2, we notice that 38 % of research prototypes do not support or at least assume secure communication while 31 % of research prototypes do not support the Assessment Function Level security (AFL) in the TAL Dimensions; 34.5 % of research prototypes also do not support or assume secure communication in the TRDL Dimensions. Proper defense techniques are needed to reliably identify malicious behaviors and mitigates such attacks in cloud environments. Some recent proposals include the header analysis approach for Denial-of-Service (DoS) attacks detection proposed in [71], the precise timing approach for identifying Man-in-the-Middle (MITM) attacks proposed in [12], and the credibility-based trust evaluation approaches proposed in [89, 102, 139, 153].

- *Scalability*: In cloud environments, the number of cloud services and their consumers is large and usually highly dynamic where new cloud services, as well as consumers, can join while others might leave the cloud environment at any time. This highly dynamic and distributed nature of cloud services requires that trust management systems to be highly scalable in order to efficiently collect feedbacks and update trust results. According to the evaluation provided in Sect. 2.4.2, 48 % of research prototypes rely on a centralized architecture for their trust management, which is not scalable and more prone to problems such as availability and security (e.g., Denial-of-Service (DoS) attack) [70]. Therefore, we believe that proper scalability and availability techniques are needed for trust management systems. Some recent work includes a decentralized approach proposed in [102] where a replication model is proposed and in [35] where load balancing techniques are used to increase the availability of the trust management system.

- *Cloud Service Discovery*: From our analysis provided in Sect. 7.3, it is clear that there is no strong evidence showing that SOC is playing an active role in the implementation and deployment of cloud services. The majority of publicly available cloud services are not based on description standards [142, 148]. There is also an urgent need for standardization especially in description languages to fully embrace cloud computing. We argue that more efficient techniques are required to overcome the cloud service discovery challenges. Fortunately, there are some attempts from the research community and some initial results have been achieved in standardization. For example, the Distributed Management Task Force (DMTF) just released, on 29 August 2012, the Cloud Infrastructure Management Interface (CIMI) specification, which standardizes interactions between cloud environments to achieve interoperable cloud infrastructure management [48].

# References

1. 10TopTenReviews. Cloud Storage Service Reviews, 2013. Accessed 05/01/2013, Available at: http://online-storage-service-review.toptenreviews.com/.
2. E. Al-Masri and Q.H. Mahmoud. Investigating Web Services on the World Wide Web. In *Proc. of the 17th Int. Conf. on World Wide Web (WWW'08)*, Beijing, China, Apr 2008.
3. J. Al-Sharawneh and M.A. Williams. Credibility-based Social Network Recommendation: Follow the Leader. In *Proc. of the 21st Australasian Conf. on Information Systems (ACIS'10)*, Brisbane, Australia, Dec 2010.
4. M. Alhamad, T. Dillon, and E. Chang. SLA-based Trust Model for Cloud Computing. In *Proc. of the 13th Int. Conf. on Network-Based Information Systems (NBiS'10)*, Takayama, Gifu, Japan, Sep 2010.
5. Amazon. Amazon.com: Online Shopping for Electronics, Apparel, Computers, Books, DVDs & More, 2011. Accessed 01/3/2011, Available at: http://www.amazon.com/.
6. Amazon-EC2. Elastic Compute Cloud (Amazon EC2), 2011. Accessed 01/04/2011, Available at: http://aws.amazon.com/ec2.
7. Amazon-S3. Amazon Simple Storage Service (Amazon - S3), 2011. Accessed 29/03/2011, Available at: http://aws.amazon.com/s3.
8. R. Aringhieri, E. Damiani, S. De Capitani di Vimercati, S. Paraboschi, and P. Samarati. Fuzzy Techniques for Trust and Reputation Management in Anonymous Peer-to-Peer Systems. *Journal of the American Society for Information Science and Technology*, 57(4):528–537, 2006.
9. R. Aringhieri, E. Damiani, S. De Capitani di Vimercati, and P. Samarati. Assessing Efficiency of Trust Management in Peer-to-Peer Systems. In *Proc. of IEEE 14th Int. Workshops on Enabling Technologies: Infrastructure for Collaborative Enterprise (WETICE'05)*, Linkoping, Sweden, Jun 2005.
10. M. Armbrust, A. Fox, R. Griffith, A.D. Joseph, R. Katz, A. Konwinski, G. Lee, D. Patterson, A. Rabkin, I. Stoica, and M. Zaharia. A View of Cloud Computing. *Communications of the ACM*, 53(4):50–58, 2010.
11. Michael Arrington. Gmail Disaster: Reports Of Mass Email Deletions, 2006. Accessed: 11/09/2010, Available at: http://techcrunch.com/2006/12/28/gmail-disaster-reports-of-mass-email-deletions/.
12. B Aziz and G Hamilton. Detecting Man-in-the-Middle Attacks by Precise Timing. In *Proc. of the 3rd Int. Conf. on Emerging Security Information, Systems and Technologies (SECURWARE'09)*, Athens/Glyfada, Greece, Jun 2009.
13. F. Azzedin and M. Maheswaran. Integrating Trust Into Grid Resource Management Systems. In *Proc. of the Int. Conf. on Parallel Processing (ICPP'02)*, Vancouver, BC, Canada, Aug 2002.

© Springer International Publishing Switzerland 2014

T. H. Noor et al., *Trust Management in Cloud Services,*

DOI 10.1007/978-3-319-12250-2

14. F. Azzedin and M. Maheswaran. Towards Trust-aware Resource Management in Grid Computing Systems. In *Proc. of the 2nd IEEE/ACM Int. Symp. on Cluster Computing and the Grid (CCGrid'02)*, Berlin, Germany, May 2002.

15. F. Azzedin and M. Maheswaran. A Trust Brokering System and its Application to Resource Management in Public-resource Grids. In *Proc. of the 18th Int. Parallel and Distributed Processing Symp. (IPDPS'04)*, Santa Fe, New Mexico, Apr 2004.

16. S. Ba and P.A. Pavlou. Evidence of the Effect of Trust Building Technology in Electronic Markets: Price Premiums and Buyer Behavior. *MIS Quarterly*, 26(3):243–268, 2002.

17. D. Bermbach, M. Klems, S. Tai, and M. Menzel. MetaStorage: A Federated Cloud Storage System to Manage Consistency-Latency Tradeoffs. In *Proc. of IEEE 4th Int. Conf. on Cloud Computing (CLOUD'11)*, Washington DC, USA, Jul 2011.

18. E. Bertino, E. Ferrari, and A. Squicciarini. Trust Negotiations: Concepts, Systems, and Languages. *Computing in Science and Engineering*, 6(4):27–34, 2004.

19. E. Bertino, F. Paci, R. Ferrini, and N. Shang. Privacy-preserving Digital Identity Management for Cloud Computing. *IEEE* Data Eng. Bull, 32(1):21–27, 2009.

20. A. Birolini. *Reliability Engineering: Theory and Practice*. Springer, 2010.

21. M. Blaze, J. Feigenbaum, and A. Keromytis. KeyNote: Trust Management for Public-key Infrastructures. In *Proc. of the 6th Int. Workshop on Security Protocols*, Cambridge, UK, Apr 1998.

22. M. Blaze, J. Feigenbaum, and J. Lacy. Decentralized Trust Management. In *Proc. of IEEE 17th Symp. on Security and Privacy (SP'96)*, Oakland, CA, USA, May 1996.

23. M. Blaze, J. Feigenbaum, and M. Strauss. Compliance Checking in the PolicyMaker Trust Management System. In *Proc. of the 2nd Int. Conf. on Financial Cryptography (FC'98)*, Anguilla, BWI, Feb 1998.

24. M. Blaze, J. Ioannidis, and A. Keromytis. Trust Management and Network Layer Security Protocols. In *Proc. of the 7th Int. Workshop on Security Protocols*, London, UK, Apr 2000.

25. Matt Blaze, Joan Feigenbaum, John Ioannidis, and Angelos D. Keromytis. . *Secure Internet Programming*, chapter The Role of Trust Management in Distributed Systems Security, pages 185–210. Springer-Verlag, London, UK, 1999.

26. Ivona Brandic, Schahram Dustdar, Tobias Anstett, David Schumm, Frank Leymann, and Ralf Konrad. Compliant Cloud Computing (C3): Architecture and Language Support for User-Driven Compliance Management in Clouds. In *Proc. of IEEE 3rd Int. Conf. on Cloud Computing (CLOUD'10)*, Miami, Florida, USA, Jul 2010.

27. R. Buyya, C.S. Yeo, and S. Venugopal. Market-oriented Cloud Computing: Vision, Hype, and Reality for Delivering it Services as Computing Utilities. In *Proc. of IEEE 10th Int. Conf. on High Performance Computing and Communications (HPCC'08)*, Dalian, China, Sep 2008.

28. J. Camenisch and E. Van Herreweghen. Design and Implementation of the Idemix Anonymous Credential System. In *Proc. of the 9th ACM Conf. on Computer and Communications Security (CCS'02)*, Washingtion, DC, USA, Nov 2002.

29. S Cantor, J Kemp, R Philpott, and E Maler. Assertions and Protocols for the OASIS Security Assertion Markup Language (saml) v2. 0, Mar 2005. Accessed 7/3/2010, Available at: http://docs.oasis-open.org/security/saml/v2.0/saml-core-2.0-os.pdf.

30. A. Cavoukian. Privacy in the clouds. *Identity in the Information Society*, 1(1):89–108, 2008.

31. K. Chen, K. Hwang, and G. Chen. Heuristic Discovery of Role-Based Trust Chains in Peer-to-Peer Networks. *IEEE Transactions on Parallel and Distributed Systems*, 20(1):83–96, 2008.

32. I.L. Child. The Psychological Meaning of Aesthetic Judgments. *Visual Arts Research*, 9(2 (18)):51–59, 1983.

33. KP Clark, ME Warnier, FMT Brazier, and TB Quillinan. Secure Monitoring of Service Level Agreements. In *Proc. of the 5th Int. Conf. on Availability, Reliability, and Security (ARES'10)*, Krakow, Poland, Feb 2010.

34. cloud9carwash. cloud9carwash, 2013. Accessed 03/04/2013, Available at: http://www.cloud9carwash.com/.

35. W Conner, A Iyengar, T Mikalsen, I Rouvellou, and K Nahrstedt. A Trust Management Framework for Service-Oriented Environments. In *Proc. of the 18th Int. Conf. on World Wide Web (WWW'09)*, Madrid, Spain, Apr 2009.

36. D Cooper, S Santesson, S Farrell, S Boeyen, R Housley, and W Polk. RFC 5280 - Internet X.509 Public Key Infrastructure Certificate and Certificate Revocation List (CRL) Profile, May 2008. Accessed: 19/04/2010, Available at: http://tools.ietf.org/html/rfc5280.

37. Oracle Corporation. Java SE 7 Remote Method Invocation (RMI) - Related APIs & Developer Guides, 2012. Accessed 11/10/2012, Available at: http://docs.oracle.com/javase/7/docs/technotes/guides/rmi/index.html.

38. Oracle Corporation. NetBeans IDE, 2013. Accessed 11/03/2013, Available at: https://netbeans.org/.

39. Crawler4j. Open Source Web Crawler for Java, 2012. Accessed 14/06/2012, Available at: http://code.google.com/p/crawler4j/.

40. Inc. Cybozu Labs. Language Detection Library for Java, 2011. Accessed 10/03/2013, Available at: http://code.google.com/p/language-detection/.

41. E. Damiani, S. De Capitani di Vimercati, S. Paraboschi, and P. Samarati. Managing and sharing servents' reputations in p2p systems. *IEEE Transactions on Knowledge and Data Engineering*, 15(4):840–854, 2003.

42. E. Damiani, S. De Capitani di Vimercati, S. Paraboschi, P. Samarati, and F. Violante. A Reputation-Based Approach for Choosing Reliable Resources in Peer-to-Peer Networks. In *Proc. of the 9th ACM Conf. on Computer and Communications Security (CCS'02)*, Washington, DC, USA, Nov 2002.

43. Olivier David and Chiffelle Jaquet. Trust and Identification in the Light of Virtual Persons, Jun 2009. Accessed 10/3/2011, Available at: http://www.fidis.net/resources/deliverables/identity-of-identity/.

44. S. De Capitani di Vimercati, S. Foresti, S. Jajodia, S. Paraboschi, G. Psaila, and P. Samarati. Integrating Trust Management and Access Control in Data-Intensive Web Applications. *ACM Transactions on the Web (TWEB)*, 6(2):1–44, 2012.

45. C. Dellarocas. The Digitization of Word of Mouth: Promise and Challenges of Online Feedback Mechanisms. *Management Science*, 49(10):1407–1424, 2003.

46. Frank Dickmann and et al. Technology Transfer of Dynamic it Outsourcing Requires Security Measures in SLAs. In *Proc. of the 7th Int. Workshop on the Economics and Business of Grids, Clouds, Systems, and Services (GECON'10)*, Ischia, Italy, Aug 2010.

47. Tharam Dillon, Chen Wu, and Elizabeth Chang. Cloud Computing: Issues and Challenges. In *Proc. of the 24th IEEE Int. Conf. on Advanced Information Networking and Applications (AINA'10)*, Perth, Australia, Apr 2010.

48. DMTF.org. DMTF Releases Specification for Simplifying Cloud Infrastructure Management, Aug 2012. Accessed: 25/11/2012, Available at: http://www.dmtf.org/news/pr/2012/8/dmtf-releases-specification-simplifying-cloud-infrastructure-management.

49. P. Domingues, B. Sousa, and L. Moura Silva. Sabotage-tolerance and Trust Management in Desktop Grid Computing. *Future Generation Computer Systems: The Int. Journal of Grid Computing and eScience*, 23(7):904–912, 2007.

50. J. R. Douceur. The Sybil Attack. In *Proc. of the 1st Int. Workshop on Peer-to-Peer Systems (IPTPS'02)*, Cambridge, MA, USA, Mar 2002.

51. Dropbox. Dropbox, 2012. Accessed 03/10/2012, Available at: http://www.dropbox.com/.

52. eBay. ebay - new & used electronics, cars, apparel, collectibles, sporting goods & more at low prices, 2011. Accessed 01/3/2011, Available at: http://www.ebay.com/.

53. C. Ellison, B. Frantz, B. Lampson, R. Rivest, B. Thomas, and T. Ylonen. SPKI Certificate Theory, 1999.

54. C.M. Ellison. Establishing Identity Without Certification Authorities. In *Proc. of the 6th Conf. on USENIX Security Symposium (SSYM'96), Focusing on Applications of Cryptography-Volume 6*, San Jose, CA, USA, Jul 1996.

55. Epinions.com. Reviews from epinions, 2011. Accessed 01/3/2011, Available at: http://www1. epinions.com/.

56. Henrik Falck. What Language is This, 2013. Accessed 10/03/2013, Available at: http:// whatlanguageisthis.com/.

57. C. Fehling, T. Ewald, F. Leymann, M. Pauly, J. Rutschlin, and D. Schumm. Capturing Cloud Computing Knowledge and Experience in Patterns. In *Proc. of IEEE 5th Int. Conf. on Cloud Computing (CLOUD'12)*, Honolulu, Hawaii, USA, Jun 2012.

58. I. Foster, Yong Zhao, I. Raicu, and S. Lu. Cloud Computing and Grid Computing 360-degree Compared. In *Proc. of Grid Computing Environments Workshop (GCE'08)*, Texas, USA, Nov 2008.

59. E. Friedman, P. Resnick, and R. Sami. *Algorithmic Game Theory*, chapter Manipulation-Resistant Reputation Systems, pages 677–697. Cambridge University Press, New York, USA, 2007.

60. B. Fung, K. Wang, R. Chen, and P.S. Yu. Privacy-preserving Data Publishing: A Survey of Recent Developments. *ACM Computing Surveys (CSUR)*, 42(4):1–53, 2010.

61. Google. Google Chart Tools, 2012. Accessed 24/02/2013, Available at: https://developers. google.com/chart/.

62. Google-Apps. Google Apps, 2011. Accessed 03/04/2011, Available at: http://www.google. com/apps/.

63. Google-Docs. Google Docs - Online documents, spreadsheets, presentations, surveys, file storage and more, 2011. Accessed 11/04/2011, Available at: https://docs.google.com/.

64. Derek Gottfrid. Self-Service, Prorated Supercomputing Fun. *The New York Times*, Nov 2007. Accessed: 20/04/2011, Available at: http://open.blogs.nytimes.com/2007/11/01/self-service-prorated-super-computing-fun/.

65. H. Guo, J. Huai, Y. Li, and T. Deng. KAF: Kalman Filter Based Adaptive Maintenance for Dependability of Composite Services. In *Proc. of the 20th Int. Conf. on Advanced Information Systems Engineering (CAiSE'08)*, Montpellier, France, June 2008.

66. S.M. Habib, S. Ries, S. Hauke, and M. Muhlhauser. Fusion of Opinions under Uncertainty and Conflict - Application to Trust Assessment for Cloud Marketplaces. In *Proc. of IEEE 11th Int. Conf. on Trust, Security and Privacy in Computing and Communications (TrustCom'12)*, Liverpool, UK, Jun 2012.

67. S.M. Habib, S. Ries, and M. Muhlhauser. Towards a Trust Management System for Cloud Computing. In *Proc. of IEEE 10th Int. Conf. on Trust, Security and Privacy in Computing and Communications (TrustCom'11)*, Changsha, China, Nov 2011.

68. M. Hausenblas, R. Grossman, A. Harth, and Cudré-Mauroux P. Large-scale Linked Data Processing - Cloud Computing to the Rescue? In *Proc. of the 2nd International Conference on Cloud Computing and Services Science (CLOSER'12)*, Porto, Portugal, Apr 2012.

69. HighCharts JS. Highcharts Interactive Javascript Charts for Your Web-page, 2012. Accessed 28/02/2013, Available at:http://www.highcharts.com/demo/.

70. K. Hoffman, D. Zage, and C. Nita-Rotaru. A Survey of Attack and Defense Techniques for Reputation Systems. *ACM Computing Surveys (CSUR)*, 42(1):1–31, 2009.

71. A. Hussain, J. Heidemann, and C. Papadopoulos. A Framework for Classifying Denial of Service Attacks. In *Proc. of the 2003 conf. on Applications, technologies, architectures, and protocols for computer communications (SIGCOMM'03)*, Karlsruhe, Germany, Aug 2003.

72. T.D. Huynh, N.R. Jennings, and N.R. Shadbolt. Certified Reputation: How an Agent Can Trust a Stranger. In *Proc. of the 5th Int. joint Conf. on Autonomous Agents and Multiagent Systems (AAMAS'06)*, Hakodate, Hokkaido, Japan, May 2006.

73. K. Hwang, S. Kulkareni, and Y. Hu. Cloud Security with Virtualized Defense and Reputation-based Trust Management. In *Proc. of IEEE 8th Int. Conf. on Dependable, Autonomic and Secure Computing (DASC'09)*, Chengdu, China, Dec 2009.

74. Kai Hwang and Deyi Li. Trusted Cloud Computing with Secure Resources and Data Coloring. *IEEE* Internet Computing, 14(5):14–22, 2010.

75. ipv6/whois. IPv6 Address whois Information Lookup Tool, 2013. Accessed 15/02/2013, Available at: http://ipduh.com/ipv6/whois/.

76. A Jøsang, R Ismail, and C Boyd. A Survey of Trust and Reputation Systems for Online Service Provision. *Decision Support Systems*, 43(2):618–644, 2007.

77. S.D. Kamvar, M.T. Schlosser, and H. Garcia-Molina. The Eigentrust Algorithm for Reputation Management in P2P Networks. In *Proc. of the 12th Int. Conf. on World Wide Web (WWW'03)*, Budapest, Hungary, May 2003.

78. Jaeyong Kang and Kwang Mong Sim. Towards Agents and Ontology for Cloud Service Discovery. In *Proc. of the 2011 Int. Conf. on Cyber-Enabled Distributed Computing and Knowledge Discovery*, Beijing, China, Oct 2011.

79. Su Myeon Kim and Marcel-Catalin Rosu. A Survey of Public Web Services. In *Proc. of the 13th Int. Conf. on World Wide Web (WWW04)*, New York, NY, USA, May 2004.

80. R.K.L. Ko, P. Jagadpramana, M. Mowbray, S. Pearson, M. Kirchberg, Q. Liang, and B.S. Lee. TrustCloud: A Framework for Accountability and Trust in Cloud Computing. In *Proc. of IEEE World Congress on Services (SERVICES'11)*, Washington, DC, USA, Jul 2011.

81. H. Koshutanski and F. Massacci. A Negotiation Scheme for Access Rights Establishment in Autonomic Communication. *Journal of Network and Systems Management*, 15(1):117–136, 2007.

82. F. Krautheim, D. Phatak, and A. Sherman. Introducing the Trusted Virtual Environment Module: A New Mechanism for Rooting Trust in Cloud Computing. In *Proc. of the 3rd Int. Conf. on Trust and Trustworthy Computing (TRUST'10)*, Berlin, Germany, Jun 2010.

83. K. Lai, M. Feldman, I. Stoica, and J. Chuang. Incentives for Cooperation in Peer-to-Peer Networks. In *Proc. of the 1st Workshop on Economics of Peer-to-Peer Systems*, Berkeley, CA, USA, Jun 2003.

84. Y. Li, Y. Liu, L. Zhang, G. Li, B. Xie, and J. Sun. An Exploratory Study of Web Services on the Internet. In *Proc. of IEEE Int. Conf. on Web Services (ICWS'07)*, Salt Lake City, Utah, USA, Jul 2007.

85. Ching Lin Vijay Varadharajan Yan Wang, and Vineet Pruthi. Enhancing Grid Security with Trust Management. In *Proc. of the 2004 IEEE Int. Conf. on Services Computing (SCC'04)*, Shanghai, China, Sep 2004.

86. G. Liu, Y. Wang, and M. Orgun. Trust Inference in Complex Trust-oriented Social Networks. In *Proc. of IEEE 12th Int. Conf. on Computational Science and Engineering (CSE'09)*, Vancouver, Canada, Aug 2009.

87. Steve Lohr. Amazon Cloud Failure Takes Down Web Sites. *The New York Times*, Apr 2011. Accessed: 29/07/2011, Available at: http://bits.blogs.nytimes.com/2011/04/21/amazon-cloud-failure-takes-down-web-sites/.

88. Jiangang Ma Quan Z. Sheng Kewen Liao Yanchun Zhang and Anne H.H. Ngu. WS-Finder: A Framework for Similarity Search of Web Services. In *Proc. of the 10th Int. Conf. on Service Oriented Computing (ICSOC'12)*, Shanghai, China, Nov 2012.

89. Z. Malik and A. Bouguettaya. Rater Credibility Assessment in Web Services Interactions. *World Wide Web*, 12(1):3–25, 2009.

90. Z. Malik and A. Bouguettaya. RATEWeb: Reputation Assessment for Trust Establishment Among Web services. *The VLDB Journal*, 18(4):885–911, 2009.

91. Z. Malik and A. Bouguettaya. Reputation Bootstrapping for Trust Establishment Among Web Services. *IEEE* Internet Computing, 13(1):40–47, 2009.

92. P.D. Manuel, S. Thamarai Selvi, and M.I.A.-E. Barr. Trust Management System for Grid and Cloud Resources. In *Proc. of the 1st Int. Conf. on Advanced Computing (ICAC'09)*, Chennai, India, Dec 2009.

93. S. Maskell and N. Gordon. A Tutorial on Particle Filters for On-line Nonlinear/Non-Gaussian Bayesian Tracking. In *Target Tracking: Algorithms and Applications (Ref. No. 2001/174), IEEE*, pages 2–1. IET, 2001.

94. Y Matsuo and H Yamamoto. Community Gravity: Measuring Bidirectional Effects by Trust and Rating on Online Social Networks. In *Proc. of the 18th Int. Conf. on World Wide Web (WWW'09)*, Madrid, Spain, Apr 2009.

95. B. Medjahed, B. Benatallah, A. Bouguettaya, A.H.H. Ngu, and A.K. Elmagarmid. Business-to-Business Interactions: Issues and Enabling Technologies. *The VLDB Journal*, 12(1):59–85, 2003.

96. Peter Mell and Timothy Grance. The NIST Definition of Cloud Computing, Sep 2011. Accessed: 05/06/2012, Available at: http://csrc.nist.gov/publications/drafts/800-145/Draft-SP-800-145_cloud-definition. pdf.

97. Michael Menzel and Rajiv Ranjan. CloudGenius: Decision Support for Web Server Cloud Migration. In *Proc. of the 21st Int. World Wide Web Conf. (WWW'12)*, Lyon, France, Apr 2012.

98. E. Meshkova, J. Riihijärvi, M. Petrova, and P. Mähönen. A Survey on Resource Discovery Mechanisms, Peer-to-Peer and Service Discovery Frameworks. *Computer networks*, 52(11):2097–2128, 2008.

99. A.N. Mian, R. Baldoni, and R. Beraldi. A Survey of Service Discovery Protocols in Mobile Ad Hoc Networks. *Pervasive Computing, IEEE*, 8(1):66–74, 2009.

100. Microsoft. Windows Live Mesh 2011, 2011. Accessed 09/05/2011, Available at: https://www.mesh.com/.

101. James H. Morris. iPad Breach Update: More Personal Data Was Potentially At Risk, 2010. Accessed: 05/05/2011, Available at: http://techcrunch.com/2010/06/15/ipad-breach-personal-data/.

102. Talal. H. Noor and Quan Z. Sheng. Credibility-Based Trust Management for Services in Cloud Environments. In *Proc. of the 9th Int. Conf. on Service Oriented Computing (ICSOC'11)*, Paphos, Cyprus, Dec 2011.

103. Talal. H. Noor and Quan Z. Sheng. Trust as a Service: A Framework for Trust Management in Cloud Environments. In *Proc. of the 12th Int. Conf. on Web and Information Systems (WISE'11)*, Sydney, Australia, Oct 2011.

104. Talal. H. Noor and Quan Z. Sheng. *Handbook on Advanced Web Services*, chapter Web Service-based Trust Management in Cloud Environments, pages 101–120. Springer, 2012.

105. Talal. H. Noor, Quan Z. Sheng, and Abdullah Alfazi. Detecting Occasional Reputation Attacks on Cloud Services. In *The 13th Int. Conf. on Web Engineering (ICWE'13)*, Aalborg, Denmark, Jul 2013.

106. Talal. H. Noor, Quan Z. Sheng, and Abdullah Alfazi. Reputation Attacks Detection for Effective Trust Assessment of Cloud Services. In *Proc. of the 12th IEEE Int. Con. on Trust, Security and Privacy in Computing and Communications (TrustCom'13)*, Melbourne, Australia, July 2013.

107. Talal. H. Noor, Quan Z. Sheng, Abdullah Alfazi, Jeriel Law, and Anne H.H. Ngu. Identifying Fake Feedback for Effective Trust Management in Cloud Environments. In *The 1st Int. Workshop on Analytics Services on the Cloud (ASC'12)*, Shanghai, China, Nov 2012.

108. Talal. H. Noor, Quan Z. Sheng, Abdullah Alfazi, Anne H.H. Ngu, and Jeriel Law. CSCE: A Crawler Engine for Cloud Services Discovery on the World Wide Web. In *The IEEE 20th Int. Conf. on Web Services (ICWS'13)*, Santa Clara Marriott, CA, USA, Jun-Jul 2013.

109. Talal. H. Noor, Quan Z. Sheng, Anne H.H. Ngu, Abdullah Alfazi, and Jeriel Law. Cloud Armor: A Platform for Credibility-Based Trust Management of Cloud Services. In *The 22nd ACM Conf. on Information and Knowledge Management (CIKM'13)*, San Francisco, CA, USA, Oct-Nov 2013.

110. Talal. H. Noor, Quan Z. Sheng, Anne H.H. Ngu, and Schahram Dustdar. Analysis of Web-Scale Cloud Services. *IEEE Internet Computing*, In press

111. Talal. H. Noor, Quan Z. Sheng, Sherali Zeadally, and Jian Yu. Trust Management of Services in Cloud Environments: Obstacles and Solutions. *ACM Computing Surveys (CSUR)*, In press

112. Oracle Corporation. MySQL, 2012. Accessed 24/07/2012, Available at: http://www.mysql.com/.

113. S. Park, L. Liu, C. Pu, M. Srivatsa, and J. Zhang. Resilient Trust Management for Web Service Integration. In *Proc. of IEEE Int. Conf. on Web Services (ICWS'05)*, Orlando, Florida, Jul 2005.

114. A. Pashalidis and C.J. Mitchell. A Taxonomy of Single Sign-on Systems. In *Proc. of the 8th Australasian Conf. on Information Security and Privacy (ACISP'03)*, Wollongong, Australia, Jul 2003.

115. S. Pearson and A. Benameur. Privacy, Security and Trust Issues Arising From Cloud Computing. In *Proc. IEEE 2nd Int. Conf. on Cloud Computing Technology and Science (CloudCom'10)*, Indianapolis, Indiana, USA, Nov - Dec 2010.

116. programmableweb.com. programmableweb, 2013. Accessed 14/03/2013, Available at: http://www.programmableweb.com/.

117. Protégé. Ontology Editor and Knowledge Acquisition System, 2013. Accessed 24/02/2013, Available at: http://protege.stanford.edu/.

118. J. Mogul H. Frystyk L. Masinter P. Leach T. Berners-Lee R. Fielding, J. Gettys. Rfc 2616: 10 status code definitions. Accessed: 29/07/2011, Available at: http://www.w3.org/Protocols/rfc2616/rfc2616-sec10.html.

119. R. Ranjan, L. Zhao, X. Wu, A. Liu, A. Quiroz, and M. Parashar. *Cloud Computing: Principles, Systems and Applications*, chapter Peer-to-Peer Cloud Provisioning: Service Discovery and Load-Balancing, pages 195–217. Springer, 2010.

120. K. Ren, C. Wang, and Q. Wang. Security Challenges for the Public Cloud. *IEEE Internet Computing*, 16(1):69–73, 2012.

121. D. Renzel, P. Schlebusch, and R. Klamma. Today's Top "RESTful" Services and Why They are not RESTful. In *Proc. of the 13th Int. Conf. on Web Information Systems Engineering (WISE'12)*, Paphos, Cyprus, Nov 2012.

122. Cloud Hosting Reviews. Cloud Hosting Reviews, 2013. Accessed 03/01/2013, Available at: http://cloudhostingreview.com.au/.

123. Eleanor Roosevelt. Facing the problems of youth. *The P.T.A. magazine: National Parent-Teacher Magazine*, 29(30):1–6, 1935.

124. Guy Rosen. Jack of All Clouds, 2011. Accessed 25/02/2011, Available at: http://www.jackofallclouds.com/2011/01/state-of-the-cloud-january-201/.

125. I. Roy, S.T.V. Setty, A. Kilzer, V. Shmatikov, and E. Witchel. Airavat: Security and Privacy for MapReduce. In *Proc. of the 7th USENIX Symp. on Networked Systems Design and Implementation (NSDI'10)*, San Jose, CA, USA, Apr 2010.

126. Jorge Salas, Francisco Perez-Sorrosal, Marta Patiño-Martínez, and Ricardo Jiménez-Peris. WS-Replication: A Framework for Highly Available Web Services. In *Proc. of the 15th Int. Conf. on World Wide Web (WWW'06)*, Edinburgh, Scotland, May 2006.

127. N. Santos, K.P. Gummadi, and R. Rodrigues. Towards Trusted Cloud Computing. In *Proc. of 2009 Workshop on Hot Topics in Cloud Computing (HotCloud'09)*, San Diego, CA, USA, Jun 2009.

128. K. Seamons, M. Winslett, and T. Yu. Limiting the Disclosure of Access Control Policies During Automated Trust Negotiation. In *Proc. of the Symp. on Network and Distributed System Security (NDSS'01)*, San Diego, CA, USA, Feb 2001.

129. Damián Serrano Marta Patiño-Martínez Ricardo Jiménez-Peris, and Bettina Kemme. An Autonomic Approach for Replication of Internet-based Services. In *Proc. of the 27th IEEE Int. Symp. on Reliable Distributed Systems (SRDS08)*, Napoli, Italy, Oct 2008.

130. Quan Z Sheng, Zakaria Maamar, Jian Yu, and Anne HH Ngu. Robust Web Services Provisioning Through On-Demand Replication. In *Proc. of the 8th Int. Conf. on Information Systems Technology and Its Applications (ISTA09)*, Sydney, Australia, Apr 2009.

131. SixXS - IPv6 Deployment & Tunnel Broker. whois IP Address Information Lookup Tool, 2013. Accessed 15/02/2013, Available at: http://www.sixxs.net/tools/whois/.

132. H Skogsrud, B Benatallah, F Casati, F Toumani, and TW Australia. Managing Impacts of Security Protocol Changes in Service-oriented Applications. In *Proc. of the 29th Int. Conf. on Software Engineering, (ICSE'07)*, Minneapolis, MN, USA, May 2007.

133. H Skogsrud, HR Motahari-Nezhad, B Benatallah, and F Casati. Modeling Trust Negotiation for Web Services. *Computer*, 42(2):54–61, 2009.

134. F Skopik, D Schall, and S Dustdar. Start Trusting Strangers? Bootstrapping and Prediction of Trust. In *Proc. of the 10th Int. Conf. on Web Information Systems Engineering (WISE'09)*. Poznan, Poland, Oct 2009.

135. F. Skopik, D. Schall, and S. Dustdar. Trustworthy Interaction Balancing in Mixed Service-Oriented Systems. In *Proc. of ACM 25th Symp. on Applied Computing (SAC'10)*, Sierre, Switzerland, Mar 2010.

136. S. Song, K. Hwang, and Y.K. Kwok. Trusted Grid Computing with Security Binding and Trust Integration. *Journal of Grid computing*, 3(1):53–73, 2005.

137. S. Song, K. Hwang, R. Zhou, and Y.K. Kwok. Trusted P2P Transactions with Fuzzy Reputation Aggregation. *IEEE Internet Computing*, 9(6):24–34, 2005.

138. B. Sotomayor, R.S. Montero, I.M. Lorente, and I. Foster. Virtual Infrastructure Management in Private and Hybrid Clouds. *IEEE Internet Computing*, 13(5):14–22, 2009.

139. M. Srivatsa and L. Liu. Securing Decentralized Reputation Management Using TrustGuard. *Journal of Parallel and Distributed Computing*, 66(9):1217–1232, 2006.

140. M. Srivatsa, L. Xiong, and L. Liu. TrustGuard: Countering Vulnerabilities in Reputation Management for Decentralized Overlay Networks. In *Proc. of the 14th Int. Conf. on World Wide Web (WWW'05)*, Chiba, Japan, May 2005.

141. The Apache Software Foundation. Apache Tomcat, 2012. Accessed 11/07/2012, Available at: http://tomcat.apache.org/.

142. Patrick Thibodeau. Frustrations with Cloud Computing Mount, 2010. Accessed: 25/11/2012, Available at: http://www.computerworld.com/s/article/9175102/.

143. Dave Thomas and Andy Hun. State Machines. *IEEE Software*, 19:10–12, 2002.

144. Hong Linh Truong Schahram Dustdar, and Kamal Bhattacharya. Programming Hybrid Services in the Cloud. In *Proc. of the 10th Int. Conf. on Service-Oriented Computing (ICSOC'12)*, Shanghai, China, Nov 2012.

145. J. Viega. Cloud Computing and the Common Man. *Computer*, 42(8):106–108, 2009.

146. Y. Wang and J. Vassileva. Toward Trust and Reputation Based Web Service Selection: A Survey. *International Transactions on Systems Science and Applications*, 3(2):118–132, 2007.

147. W. Wei, J. Du, T. Yu, and X. Gu. SecureMR: A Service Integrity Assurance Framework for MapReduce. In *Proc. of the Annual Computer Security Applications Conf. (ACSAC'09)*, Honolulu, Hawaii, USA, Dec 2009.

148. Yi. Wei and M. Brian Blake. Service-oriented Computing and Cloud Computing: Challenges and Opportunities. *Internet Computing, IEEE*, 14(6):72–75, 2010.

149. T. Weishaupl, C. Witzany, and E. Schikuta. gSET: Trust Management and Secure Accounting for Business in the Grid. In *Proc. of the 6th IEEE Int. Symp. on Cluster Computing and the Grid (CCGrid'06)*, Singapore, May 2006.

150. Jianshu Weng, Chunyan Miao, and Angela Goh. Protecting Online Rating Systems from Unfair Ratings. In *Proc. of the 2nd Int. Conf. on Trust, Privacy, and Security in Digital Business (TrustBus'05)*. Copenhagen, Denmark, Aug 2005.

151. B. White. Accessibility Challenges of the Next Decade: Cloud and Mobile Computing and Beyond. In *Proc. of the 8th Int. Cross-Disciplinary Conf. on Web Accessibility*, Hyderabad, Andhra Pradesh, India, Mar 2011.

152. L. Xiong and L. Liu. A Reputation-based Trust Model for Peer-to-Peer e-commerce Communities. In *Proc. of IEEE Int. Conf. on e-Commerce (CEC'03)*, Newport Beach, CA, USA, Jun 2003.

153. L. Xiong and L. Liu. Peertrust: Supporting Reputation-based Trust for Peer-to-Peer Electronic Communities. *IEEE Transactions on Knowledge and Data Engineering*, 16(7):843–857, 2004.

154. J. Yao, S. Chen, C. Wang, D. Levy, and J. Zic. Accountability as a Service for the Cloud. In *Proc. of IEEE Int. Conf. on Services Computing (SCC'10)*, Miami, FL, USA, Jul 2010.

155. Lina Yao and Quan Z Sheng. Particle Filtering based Availability Prediction for Web Services. In *Proc. of the 9th Int. Conf. on Service Oriented Computing (ICSOC'11)*. Paphos, Cyprus, Dec 2011.

156. C.M. Yu and K.W. Ng. A Mechanism to Make Authorization Decisions in Open Distributed Environments without Complete Policy Information. In *Proc. of the Int. Conf. on Computational Science (ICCS'06)*, Reading, UK, May 2006.

157. C.M. Yu and K.W. Ng. DPMF: A Policy Management Framework for Heterogeneous Authorization Systems in Grid Environments. *Multiagent and Grid Systems*, 5(2):235–263, 2009.

158. R. Zhou and K. Hwang. Trust Overlay Networks for Global Reputation Aggregation in P2P Grid Computing. In *Proc. of the 20th Int. Symp. on Parallel and Distributed Processing (IPDPS'06)*, Rhodes Island, Greece, Apr 2006.

159. R. Zhou and K. Hwang. Powertrust: A Robust and Scalable Reputation System for Trusted Peer-to-Peer Computing. *IEEE Transactions on Parallel and Distributed Systems*, 18(5):460–473, 2007.

160. C.N. Ziegler and J. Golbeck. Investigating Interactions of Trust and Interest Similarity. *Decision Support Systems*, 43(2):460–475, 2007.

Printed in the United States
By Bookmasters